THE LITTLE BROWN JUG

THE MICHIGAN-MINNESOTA RIVALRY

To Jake,
A true Michigan Fan!
Go Blue!
Ken Magee

Authors Ken Magee (left) and Jon Stevens pose with the Little Brown Jug at Schembechler Hall's Al Glick Field House in February 2014.

FRONT COVER: Minnesota football custodian Oscar Munson discovered the Little Brown Jug in the visitors' locker room in Minneapolis after the 1903 Michigan-Minnesota game. He began the tradition of painting each game's final score on the jug. Here, he paints the results of the 1934 contest. (Courtesy of the University of Minnesota Archives.)

COVER BACKGROUND: Before Michigan Stadium was constructed in 1927, the Wolverines hosted games at Ferry Field. This photograph shows their 1910 matchup with the Gophers. (Courtesy of the Bentley Historical Library.)

BACK COVER: This image of the Little Brown Jug was used in the 2013 Minnesota-Michigan football game program on page 14. (Courtesy of the University of Michigan Athletic Department Collection, Bentley Historical Library.)

THE LITTLE BROWN JUG

THE MICHIGAN-MINNESOTA RIVALRY

Ken Magee and Jon M. Stevens
Foreword by Glenn E. "Shemy" Schembechler III

ARCADIA
PUBLISHING

Published by Arcadia Publishing
Charleston, South Carolina

Printed in the United States of America

Library of Congress Control Number: 2014945494

For all general information, please contact Arcadia Publishing:
Telephone 843-853-2070
Fax 843-853-0044
E-mail sales@arcadiapublishing.com
For customer service and orders:
Toll-Free 1-888-313-2665

Visit us on the Internet at www.arcadiapublishing.com

Ken: To my mother, Bettie Magee, who took me to my first Wolverines game as a little boy. God Bless and Go Blue!

Jon: To my parents, Don and Peggy Stevens. Thank you for never being too busy to "have a catch." Go Blue!

CONTENTS

FOREWORD

It is difficult to fathom that my dad has not been in our midst for the better part of eight years now, but as the time has passed, his lessons about life and passion seem to still grow quickly in our hearts and minds. He is, and always will be, the greatest competitor I will ever know. That was his approach each and every day. So as we look back on our great and storied rivalry with the Minnesota Gophers, his philosophy held true, and the high regard he had for the oldest trophy in college football never wavered. His career record against Minnesota was 19-2, which is impressive on the surface, but if he were with us today, the two losses would be his most vivid memories. His respect for the Little Brown Jug grew immensely after the first Minnesota loss. Dad went on record in his own memoirs, saying, "I never realized how much the jug meant until we lost it." We had come into the game in late October 1977 as the no. 1 ranked team in the country and on a clear track to win the Big Ten championship. The game turned out to be a 16-0 white wash of Michigan that combined a much embattled Minnesota team that did not determine its starting quarterback until the morning of the game and five costly turnovers by Michigan, one of which spotted the Gophers an early 10-0 lead. It is easy to imagine Bo's response to this rare debacle, which turned out to be Michigan's lone defeat of the regular season. In similar fashion, the 1986 version had the Wolverines coming in undefeated and the second-ranked team in the country and the showdown with Ohio State the next Saturday. The game was controlled by the Gophers from start to finish, with another five turnovers given up by the Wolverines proving once again to be the deciding factor, and ended with a field goal to secure a Minnesota victory as time expired. The silver lining for each of these games is that it provided the extra motivation to lead Michigan to the Big Ten championship and trips to the Rose Bowl both times. I can hear Dad's voice again: "You either get better or you get worse, you never stay the same." What better lesson is there?

—Glenn E. "Shemy" Schembechler III

ACKNOWLEDGMENTS

Foremost, we would like to thank the thousands of men who played football and coached for these two prestigious universities. Because of you, the game is played, year after year, for over a century. A project of this magnitude utilizes images from many resources, abbreviations for the source of each image will be found at the end of each photograph caption in parentheses. We would like to thank the University of Michigan's Bentley Historical Library (BHL), specifically division head of reference Karen Jania, associate archivist Malgosia Myc, assistant archivist Emma Hawker, reference assistants Louis Miller and Diana Bachman, and archivists Greg Kinney and Brian Williams, who all provided so much to the success of this project. From the University of Minnesota's Archives (UMA), we would like to thank Erik Moore, university archivist, and Erin George, assistant archivist. To Greg Dooley of Mvictors.com (MVC), an avid researcher of this century-old water jug, your assistance helped pave the way for this book. To Mark Schlanderer (MS), who painstakingly assisted us with fact checking and provided focus for the entire project. Others from Michigan who provided input are Michael Alley, John Harrison, Bob Rosiek, Jim Parker, Chris Potter (CP), Karl and Amy Lagler, and Kurt Anderson and Jil Gordon. From Minnesota, we would like to thank the Red Wing Collectors Society Foundation and president David Hallstrom, the Red Wing Collectors Society and executive director Stacy Wegner, and society members Mark Cellotti and Stan Bougie. We also thank the Minnesota Historical Society (MHS), as well as Tom Betcher (TB) and Kathy Erickson, who opened their home and collection to us while we searched for Little Brown Jug artifacts. Also, appreciation is extended to Larry Jaehnert (LJ) and Jim and Nancy Stiller (JNS), who allowed us to view and utilize parts of their personal Minnesota collections; Al Papas Jr. (APJ), whose ability to capture Minnesota football history is superb; and Jeff Keiser of the University of Minnesota Athletic Department (UMAD). To all the professional photographers: Robert Kalmbach, who donated his collection of photographs to the Bentley Historical Library (RK-BHL); Eric Bronson of www.bronsonphoto.com; Amir Ganzu; Jonathan Knight (JK); and Joseph Arcure (JA) for their understanding that the photographs of today capture and memorialize college football's greatest moments. To Shemy Schembechler and our years of friendship. From the University of Michigan Athletic Department, our special thanks to Jon Falk, football equipment manager, for 40 years, and to Bruce Madej, for opening doors and allowing us access to Schembechler Hall to specifically view the Little Brown Jug, the holy grail of college trophies, which is normally kept under lock and key at an undisclosed location while on the Ann Arbor campus.

INTRODUCTION

What do many All-Americans, Hall of Famers, and thousands of college football players, coaches, war heroes, and a president of the United States all have in common? They have all participated in the classic rivalry football game known as the "Battle for the Little Brown Jug." This is a football contest played in Minnesota or in Michigan, where the winner earns the privilege of maintaining possession of a simple kilned water jug that has been adorned with final score results of each game since the rivalry began.

The University of Michigan and the University of Minnesota both have a long and storied football tradition dating back to the late 1800s. Over a century of history exists between these two schools of playing on the gridiron from the earliest, formative years of the sport to the evolution seen in today's game. It only seems natural that there should be something special about the two teams when they play each other. That something special started in 1903 after a brutal football game between two of the nation's top teams. The Michigan Wolverines and the Minnesota Gophers played to a final score of 6-6. From a football standpoint, the game was of great national interest, and football fans around the country clamored for details surrounding the outcome. The simple act of a University of Minnesota custodian finding a Red Wing earthenware water jug discarded after the game by the Michigan team would become a symbolic rivalry trophy emulated by others and embraced by all of college football to this day.

Coaches and players draw on tradition as motivation to excel and to build upon their successes and failures. The Little Brown Jug trophy is a most forceful motivator in the Minnesota- Michigan game. The Little Brown Jug tradition was first established by Minnesota coach Henry "Doc" Williams and Michigan coach Fielding Yost. It was then strongly embraced by Coaches Bierman and Crisler, followed by Coaches Warmath and Schembechler, who both built upon it greatly. Several other coaches have followed suit, and to this day Coaches Kill and Hoke continue to stress the Little Brown Jug's importance for success.

Today's college football fans often view the historic rivalry between Michigan and Ohio State football teams as one of significant importance. Although true, as the win or loss of this and any other game have specific ramifications, it is the Michigan-Minnesota game that overshadowed college football for much of the first half of the 20th century. During the first 50 years of the 1900s, the outcome of the Little Brown Jug game would often be a major contributing factor as to who won the national championship.

As storied as the Little Brown Jug is, so are the nicknames and fight songs. The team nicknames, the Wolverines of Michigan and the Gophers of Minnesota, have lore attached to both universities. "Wolverines" has been has been used since the 1860s. Michigan is known as the "Wolverine State," and there are several theories as to its original designation for both the state and the university. They range from when the French settled Michigan in the 1700s to a battle over the border dispute between Michigan and Ohio in 1803. One thing for certain is that a wild wolverine in the state of Michigan is a rare occurrence, and there has never been an example of skeletal remains or trapping of a live wolverine in Michigan modern times. Only one time since the 1800s, in 2004, has a wolverine been verified as living in the wild in the state. Coach Yost embraced the nickname and even went as far as to bring live, caged wolverines from the Detroit Zoo to Michigan Stadium in 1927 to parade in front of the spectators.

The Gophers of Minnesota has been used for over a century and also celebrates the state's nickname: the "Gopher State." The phrase "Golden Gophers" is used interchangeably now but was not adopted until the 1930s, when legendary radio announcer Halsey Hall coined the moniker "Golden Gophers," as the team wore all-gold uniforms while playing on the gridiron.

Even the fight songs of both schools conjure up images of yesteryear. Michigan student Louis Elbel penned its fight song "The Victors" after a major victory over the University of Chicago in 1898. Elbel was traveling home to Ann Arbor on a train after the game when he completed the lyrics. The following spring, John Philip Sousa and his band traveled to Ann Arbor to perform at University Hall, and Elbel provided a copy of the music to Sousa, who had his band perform "The Victors" for its initial debut on April 8, 1899. Minnesota wished to replace its hymn-like song "Hail Minnesota" with a more suitable chorus related to football. The *Minnesota Daily* and *Minneapolis Tribune* sponsored a public contest to develop a new fight song. The winning composer was Floyd Hutsell, who dedicated his "Minnesota Rouser" fight song to B.A. Rose, the bandmaster at the University of Minnesota. The fight song was first published on November 21, 1909, in the *Minneapolis Tribune* and echoes Minnesota's historic cheer "Ski-U-Mah" during its verse. History has proven that after every hard-fought battle, whether it is the Wolverines or the Gophers who are victorious, the Little Brown Jug will be hoisted into the air while the winners proudly sing their fight song.

Similar to many historic figures, the Little Brown Jug has not been immune to exaggerated stories and folklore. For years, it was thought that the Wolverines traveled with the Little Brown Jug from Ann Arbor to carry their own personal water supply free of suspicion, when in fact it was simply purchased in Minneapolis prior to the game. It was widely reported for decades that the rivalry began when Michigan coach Fielding Yost wrote to the Gophers and asked for the jug to be returned. In actuality, Yost was not even aware that Michigan had left the jug behind, nor would he have cared, given the low value (30¢ cost) of the jug relative to Michigan's gate receipts of $13,000 from the 1903 game. In actuality, Minnesota's Doc Cooke was interested in generating more spectator interest for the 1909 game and came up with the idea of using the discarded water jug as a trophy for the game winner. Cooke proposed to Yost the idea of challenging Michigan to win back their water jug. Always enthusiastic, Yost agreed, thus giving birth to college football's first rivalry trophy. Credit for dispelling the inaccurate myths about the Little Brown Jug should go to noted Michigan football historian Greg Dooley, who has spent considerable time researching the true history of the Little Brown Jug. Dooley also notes that the name itself, the "Little Brown Jug" is a myth. It is not little, standing almost 16 inches tall with a circumference of 37 inches and weighing more than 20 pounds, nor was it originally brown. Nevertheless, the Little Brown Jug is the pinnacle of all college football trophies.

The 101st game and next battle for the Little Brown Jug between the Michigan Wolverines and the Minnesota Gophers will be held in Michigan Stadium on September 27, 2014.

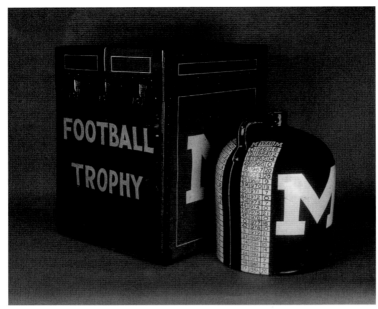

The Little Brown Jug—the grandfather of all rivalry trophies—and its trophy case are shown here. The Little Brown Jug is the genesis of well over 100 different rivalry trophy contests played each season between many schools across the various divisions of NCAA college football. (JA.)

Jon Falk, Michigan's "Keeper of the Little Brown Jug" and equipment manager for 40 years, and himself a part of Michigan football tradition, closes the lid on the Little Brown Jug trophy case for the final time before his retirement in 2014. Jon said about his arrival in 1974, "Bo told me, 'You have three main duties: one, protect the Little Brown Jug; two, protect the Paul Bunyan trophy; and three, help the Michigan football team win the Big Ten championship.' I am proud that I did my job well for 40 years." (Photograph by Jon M. Stevens.)

1

PRE-1903

BEFORE THE BATTLE
FOR THE JUG

The first football contest between the University of Michigan Wolverines and the University of Minnesota Gophers was played on October 17, 1892, in Minneapolis, Minnesota; the Gophers defeated the Wolverines 14-6. The following year, Minnesota traveled to Ann Arbor and again was victorious 34-20. The Wolverines won the next four contests, as year after year the two teams gained momentum in skill and reputation. This led to a showdown in 1903, and both teams were considered the powerhouse football teams of the Midwest as well as top teams in the country.

In 1861, near Red Wing, Minnesota, a German immigrant named John Paul is credited with discovering that the clay surrounding the Red Wing area was excellent for making utilitarian pottery ware, such as crocks, churns, and jugs. In 1878, a group of citizens formed the Red Wing Stoneware Company that later used the logo of a Red Wing stamped on the various styles of kilned pieces. At the time, it would have been impossible to believe that a zinc-glazed, five-gallon, putty-colored, earthen jug would become such a celebrated part of college football history.

This undated photograph shows Red Wing Stoneware Company employees with finished five-gallon jugs that are the same style of what would someday be known as the Little Brown Jug. (The Red Wing Collectors Society.)

This is an early-1900s pennant for both Michigan and Minnesota, depicting the colors of the two schools. It is currently on loan to the University of Michigan Football Museum at Schembechler Hall and is displayed in the exhibit section dedicated to the rivalry between Michigan and Minnesota. (Ken Magee collection.)

Shown is a game program from the 1895 contest played at Base Ball Park in Detroit, Michigan. The Wolverines were victorious 20-0 in front of 3,500 spectators. It was Michigan's first victory over Minnesota en route to an 8-1 season record. (BHL.)

This game program is from the 1897 game played at DAC Park in Detroit, Michigan, with a photograph of Michigan captain James R. Hogg. The final score of Michigan's 14-0 victory is penciled on the cover. (Ken Magee collection.)

In 1902, Michigan captain Harrison S. "Boss" Weeks zeroes in on a Minnesota player with the ball in the first-ever Michigan-Minnesota game played in Ann Arbor. It was the 22nd consecutive victory for Fielding Yost since his arrival at Michigan and the first time he had faced Coach Williams in their storied rivalry. (BHL.)

This 1902 game action photograph shows Minnesota executing a cross-block play. Notice how Coach Yost and trainer Keane Fitzpatrick are both on the playing field, close to the game action. (BHL.)

PRE-1903: BEFORE THE BATTLE FOR THE JUG

2

1903 – 1909

The Rivalry Begins

Head coach Fielding Yost's defending national champion Wolverines traveled to Minneapolis in 1903 to battle the Gophers in what was billed by the *New York Times* as "one of the most desperate games in years." Minnesota coach Dr. Henry "Doc" Williams's team was the underdog despite a 7-0 record and outscoring their opponents 506-6. Before the game, Yost had concerns Minnesota might "dope" the water supply and sent a student manager, Tommy Roberts, to purchase a water jug to ensure the water would be free of suspicion. Roberts spent 30¢ on a five-gallon Red Wing jug that would soon become part of football history.

Minnesota dominated the Wolverines in almost every statistical category except one—points scored—which resulted in a final tie score of 6-6 after Minnesota scored a touchdown with two minutes left on the clock. Many of the 20,000 jubilant Minnesota fans stormed the field, thus causing the game to be ended two minutes early. The Gophers and college football pundits considered the tie game to be a major upset over the Wolverines. It proved to be the first game in Yost's tenure as Michigan's head coach where he was not victorious in a football contest.

The following morning, a custodian named Oscar Munson, while cleaning the visitors' locker room in the University of Minnesota Armory, discovered the discarded water jug. Munson took the jug to athletic director Dr. Louis J. "Doc" Cooke, where Munson proclaimed in his strong Scandinavian accent, "Look Doc, Jost left his yug!" Cooke retained the jug, and he and Munson proudly inscribed on it in large print "Minnesota 6" and in small print "Michigan 6." As a footnote, they added, "Michigan Jug captured by Oscar October 31, 1903." The jug was then suspended from Doc Cooke's office ceiling, where it remained in plain view.

The 1903 game was so brutal that it was not until 1909 when the two teams faced each other again in Minnesota. The morning before the 1909 game, a pep rally was planned for both teams. Minnesota's All-American captain, John McGovern, was instructed by Doc Cooke, "You tell that Michigan captain they can have their jug back if they beat us tomorrow." Michigan accepted the challenge and defeated the Gophers 15-6. They returned to Ann Arbor victorious, with the jug, thus beginning college football's first football trophy game.

AND THE DISCUSSION IS PURELY ACADEMIC.

Here is a cartoon illustration before the 1903 game in Minneapolis. (BHL.)

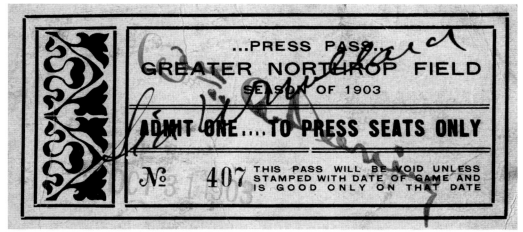

This press pass ticket to Greater Northrop Field in Minneapolis permitted access to one of the greatest football contests ever played, up to that time, in the history of college football. (BHL.)

This is the game program for the 1903 battle between Michigan and Minnesota. The final score was a tie, 6-6. It was considered an upset over the Wolverines, who had won 29 consecutive games to that point and were two-time defending national champions. It would be another two years before Michigan lost a game. (UMA.)

FIELDING H. YOST

Coach Fielding H. Yost arrived at Michigan in 1901 after coaching at Ohio Wesleyan (1897), Nebraska (1898), Kansas (1899), and Stanford (1900). From 1901 to 1905 at Michigan, his coaching record was 55-1-1. His career overall record at Michigan was 165-29-10. Yost won six national championships and 10 Western (Big Ten) Conference championships. He was inducted into the College Football Hall of Fame in 1951. (MS.)

DR. H. L. WILLIAMS, Coach

Henry "Doc" Williams played football at Yale alongside legends Amos Alonzo Stagg and William Walter "Pudge" Heffelfinger. Williams coached Minnesota from 1900 to 1921 and led Minnesota to one national championship (1904, shared with Michigan) and eight Western Conference championships. (MS.)

Minnesota captain Ed Rogers led the Gophers in the 1903 historic tie game. His drop kick extra point was the sixth and final deciding point. Rogers, a Native American, had previously played end for six years at Carlisle and was the team captain. He was inducted in to the College Football Hall of Fame in 1968. (UMA.)

Willie Heston, Michigan's legendary running back, had scored two touchdowns in the 1902 game but was held scoreless in the 1903 game. Fifty years later, Heston stated, "The 1903 contest was the hardest contested game in which I ever played." He scored 72 career touchdowns—still a Michigan record. He was elected to the College Football Hall of Fame in 1954. (BHL.)

Fred Schacht, Minnesota's first All-American player, was the heaviest lineman, at tackle, weighing 210 pounds. In that era, tackles could be used to carry the football. It is no surprise that Schacht was known for his ability also as a power runner. He was the running spearhead for the last scoring drive leading to the Minnesota five-point touchdown by Egil Boeckmann in 1903. (UMA.)

This postcard shows Greater Northrop Field during the 1903 game. (LJ.)

Here is Greater Northrop Field during the 1903 game. Note the spectators who have climbed high into the trees to watch the action. Northrop Field was the Gophers' home field from 1899 to 1923. (UMA.)

Michigan's Tom Hammond kicks the extra point to give Michigan a 6-0 lead after Joe Maddock had scored Michigan's lone touchdown in the 1903 game. (BHL.)

This newspaper headline is from the November 1, 1903, issue of the *Minneapolis Sunday Tribune* the day following the historic 1903 football contest. (MVC.)

A contemporary image shows the University of Minnesota Armory, where the jug was found by Oscar Munson the day after the 1903 game. (MVC.)

Custodian Oscar Munson found the jug discarded by the Wolverines after the 1903 game. This photograph was taken after Doc Cooke had painted the jug and forever memorialized Munson's place in college football lore. (BHL.)

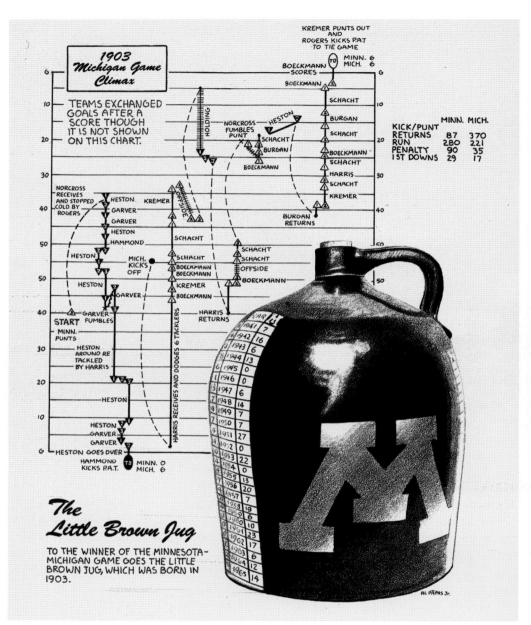

A pen-and-ink drawing by noted Minnesota artist Al Papas Jr. depicts the play-by-play scoring game chart for the two scores made in the 1903 contest. The artwork is provided compliments of Al Papas Jr. and the University of Minnesota Press from the publication *Gophers Illustrated*. Note that the Michigan touchdown credited to Willie Heston was later changed by historians to give proper credit to Joe Maddock. (APJ.)

The Little Brown Jug hangs suspended from Doc Cooke's ceiling after it was painted by Cooke and Oscar Munson following the 1903 game. Years later, Cooke mused, "I sometimes think the jug has been filled with spirits, not alcoholic, but the disembodied spirits of the countless players who have fought for it on the gridiron." (UMA.)

Souvenir Program

Minnesota-Michigan

Foot-Ball Game

Nov. 20, 1909

CAPT. McGOVERN

This game program dates from the 1909 contest at Northrop Field. It was the first game played between the two teams since the brutal battle on the gridiron in 1903. History proved this to be the first rival trophy game in college football history. Michigan was victorious, 15-6. (UMA.)

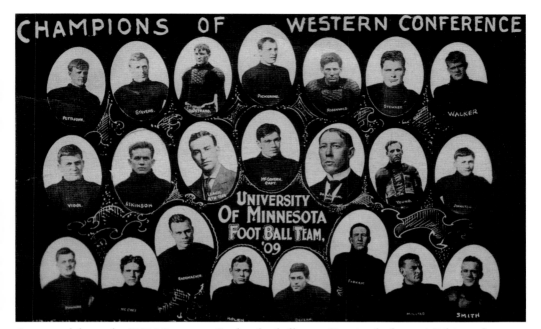

A postcard shows the 1909 Minnesota Gopher football team. Despite the loss to Michigan that year, Minnesota was still the Western Conference champion with an overall record of 6-1. At the time, Michigan had voluntarily withdrawn from the Western Conference, from 1907 to 1917. (UMA.)

Official Line-up

MICHIGAN vs. MINNESOTA

Northrop Field, Saturday, November 20

Quarterback John McGovern is not listed on this lineup scorecard of the 1909 contest. McGovern had been injured and was questionable for the game. As it turned out, he was able to play in the game. (Ken Magee collection.)

MICHIGAN		MINNESOTA
CONKLIN	L. E.	VIDAL—SCHAIN
CASEY	L. T.	WALKER
BENBROOK	L. G.	MOHLSTAD
SMITH	C.	FARNAM
EDMUNDS	R. G.	POWERS
WELLS	R. T.	McCREE
PATTENGILL	R. E.	RADEMACHER
RANNEY		
MILLER	Q. B.	ATKINSON
MAGIDSOHN	L. H.	ROSENWALD
ALLERDICE (capt.	R. H.	STEVENS
CLARK	F. B.	PICKERING

Minnesota All-American quarterback and team captain John McGovern played with a broken collar bone in the 1909 game. Coach Yost, as an act of friendship to Doc Cooke, ensured that the Michigan players would not purposely aggravate the injury during the game. McGovern is also credited with delivering Doc Cooke's challenge to Michigan about winning the jug. McGovern was elected to the College Football Hall of Fame in 1966. (UMA.)

Shown here are 1909 Michigan captain David Allerdice (with football) and Coach Yost. (BHL.)

These game-action photographs depict the 1909 Michigan victory, 15-6. As the students played for school pride and personal honor, there is no way they could have fathomed this game would become the first trophy game in college football. It started a tradition in college football that would lead to many other trophy rivalry games throughout the country. The next Western Conference trophy games started in 1925. The Illibuck trophy was established between Illinois and Ohio State, and the Old Oaken Bucket trophy was for the winner of the annual Indiana and Purdue rivalry. (Both, *Michiganensian* yearbook.)

A close-up photograph reveals the original form and putty color of the jug. It was painted brown in 1920 with the two school block M's and the scores of each game, creating the moniker "the Little Brown Jug." (BHL.)

3

1910 − 1933

MICHIGAN TAKES CHARGE

The 1910 contest was legendary for the introduction of various tactics to the game of college football. Coach Williams introduced his famous "Minnesota Shift." Coach Yost countered Coach Williams's shift by introducing a tactic that used the new rule allowing a player to pass the football. This was the first time in a major college football game where a championship was decided by the "newfangled" forward pass. Ironically, it had been Coach Williams who six years previously had proposed the rule change to allow the forward pass. That year, it was the first game played for the Little Brown Jug in Ann Arbor. The contest also marked the last time the rivalry was played until 1919. Michigan had withdrawn from the Western Conference in 1907 due to Coach Yost not wanting to adhere to a restrictive playing schedule. Michigan rejoined the conference in 1917, allowing the rivalry to continue two years later.

In 1919, the Little Brown Jug was won by Minnesota for the first time. It was after the 1920 Michigan victory that Coach Yost proposed the putty-colored water jug trophy be hand-painted with black scores on the surface. The jug was also painted from its original color of putty to brown and was adorned with the two school block M's. Columns were created for the final scores of each game to be inscribed. The decision to paint the jug portrays the image of how the Little Brown Jug appears to this day. Including 1920 and over the next 13 years, Michigan won 12 times, Minnesota won once, and there was one tie. Michigan won the national championship four times, from 1910 to 1933, of which three would have been derailed with a loss to Minnesota.

The 1933 national champion Michigan squad tied its game with Minnesota in what became a prelude of change in the following decade for Minnesota. It was near the end of this period that an interesting chapter in the existence of the Little Brown Jug unfolded. In 1931, the jug was stolen from Michigan's campus. Shortly thereafter, an imitation Little Brown Jug was recovered and portrayed as the original. It was not until two years later that the real Little Brown Jug was retrieved. The trophy has since has been closely guarded by the holding university.

This large broadside poster promotes the 1910 game played in Ann Arbor. Two-time All-American and Michigan team captain Al Benbrook is portrayed here. The 1910 game was the first played in Ann Arbor when the two teams dueled for the Little Brown Jug. Michigan was victorious, 6-0. (BHL.)

Eighteen thousand spectators purchased a ticket to the 1910 game in which the winner would be proclaimed "Champion of America." The game featured Coach Williams's newly developed and famous Minnesota Shift, which was used before a play starts to keep the opposing defense off balance. Coach Yost countered these tactics with the forward pass to win the 1910 game 6-0. Ironically, it was Coach Williams who proposed allowing the forward pass in 1904, but the rule change did not take effect until 1906. (At right, MS; below, Ken Magee collection.)

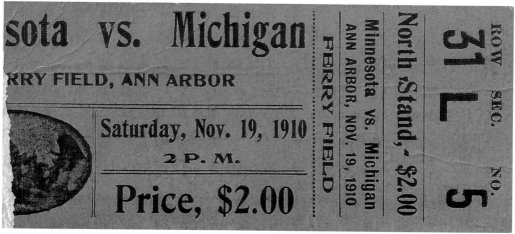

Michigan All-American Stanfield Wells scored the victorious Michigan team's only touchdown in 1910 by following 265-pound captain Al Benbrook into the end zone from the one-yard line. This scoring play occurred near the end of the game following two consecutive long forward passes by Wells to end Stan Borleske that completely surprised the Minnesota defense. (BHL.)

In the 1910 game, Minnesota All-American Jim Walker blocked a Michigan punt, and his teammate Len Frank scooped up the football and ran for a touchdown. The touchdown was immediately called back because it was ruled that an official had touched the ball while it was in play. (UMA.)

1910–1933: MICHIGAN TAKES CHARGE

A photograph of Ferry Field shows the action during the 1910 game between the Gophers and the Wolverines. Ferry Field was Michigan's home from 1906 through 1926. The Wolverines would move to the newly constructed Michigan Stadium for the 1927 season. (BHL.)

Michigan fullback George Lawton carries the football in the 1910 game in which the Wolverines upset the mighty Gophers 6-0 and gave Minnesota its only loss of the season. (BHL.)

For big games, it was common for the two opposing teams to have a dinner banquet together the night before. This provided a venue for a commentary by the players, captains, and coaches. (Ken Magee collection.)

The *Michigan Daily* headline the day after the contest crowning the Wolverines reads, "Champions of America." Clark Shaughnessy, who later was credited as the father of the T-formation, viewed the game as a substitute on the Minnesota bench. Years later, he wrote, "The 1910 game was the greatest game he ever saw, unmatched for power on the field and drama of opposing tactics by the coaches." (BHL.)

Dr. Henry L. "Doc" Williams waited almost two decades to secure a Minnesota victory and secure the Little Brown Jug. In 1919, his team demolished the Wolverines 34-7 at Ferry Field in Ann Arbor. (UMA.)

Minnesota star halfback Arnie Oss scored three touchdowns in the 1919 game, including a 63-yard run for the final score of the day. These three touchdowns are still a Minnesota scoring record versus Michigan. (UMA.)

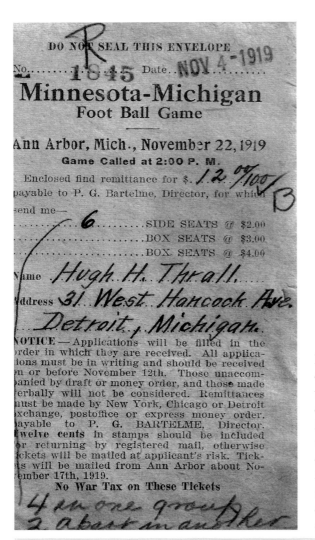

DO NOT SEAL THIS ENVELOPE

No...... 1845 Date. NOV 4 - 1919

Minnesota-Michigan
Foot Ball Game

Ann Arbor, Mich., November 22, 1919
Game Called at 2:00 P. M.

Enclosed find remittance for $. 12 %/100
payable to P. G. Bartelme, Director, for which
send me—

.......6........SIDE SEATS @ $2.00
..............BOX SEATS @ $3.00
..............BOX SEATS @ $4.00

Name Hugh H. Thrall

Address 31 West Hancock Ave.
Detroit, Michigan.

NOTICE — Applications will be filled in the
order in which they are received. All applications must be in writing and should be received
on or before November 12th. Those unaccom-
panied by draft or money order, and those made
verbally will not be considered. Remittances
must be made by New York, Chicago or Detroit
exchange, postoffice or express money order,
payable to P. G. BARTELME, Director.
Twelve cents in stamps should be included
for returning by registered mail, otherwise
tickets will be mailed at applicant's risk. Tickets will be mailed from Ann Arbor about November 17th, 1919.

No War Tax on These Tickets

4 in one group
2 apart in another

Here are the ticket and ticket-order envelope to the 1919 contest. This was the most widely attended game of the year for the Wolverines, with 30,000 fans. Despite all the support for the Wolverines, the mighty Gophers clearly dominated the game, winning 34-7. Coach Yost's record was 3-4 for the 1919 season, his only losing record during his 25 years as Michigan's head coach. (Both, Ken Magee collection.)

THE MICHIGAN JUG HOME AGAIN

Following the 1919 game, Doc Cooke continued the tradition of painting the score on the Little Brown Jug by adding the 1919 game score. This photograph is taken from the Minnesota 1921 yearbook and still refers to the jug as the "Michigan Jug." (UMA.)

No longer attached to Doc Cooke's ceiling, Minnesota was clearly pleased with its stomping of Michigan and proudly displayed the "Michigan Jug" for all to see. (UMA.)

Michigan-Minnesota Jug brought back to Ann Arbor by Minnesota's defeat last November.

It was suggested by Coach Yost that the jug be painted with the two different styles of block M's for each school. Yost also suggested a running account of each game score. His suggestions were implemented, and the Little Brown Jug was painted after the return to Ann Arbor from Minnesota in 1920 following Michigan's 3-0 victory. (BHL.)

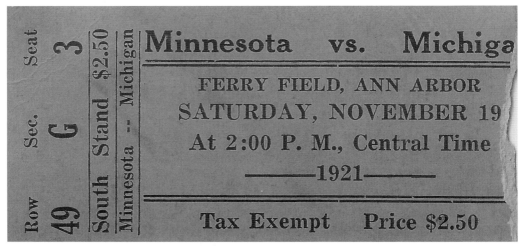

The 1921 contest was Doc Williams's final game as head coach against Michigan. Although he was a close friend of Coach Yost, the Wolverines pulverized the Gophers 38-0. (Ken Magee collection.)

1910–1933: MICHIGAN TAKES CHARGE

At the 1921 game in Ann Arbor at Ferry Field, Michigan fans form a block M with a light blue color. Michigan cheerleader Al Cuthbert stands by to rally support for the Wolverines. (BHL.)

Coach Yost (right) and 1922 All-American captain Paul Goebel get ready to board the train to Minneapolis with the Little Brown Jug. The megaphone with a *W* belonged to the Wisconsin Badgers, who had lost the previous week while playing in Ann Arbor. The megaphone was left behind by Wisconsin after the game. While en route to Minneapolis, Coach Yost delivered the megaphone to a representative of the Badgers that was in Chicago during Michigan's train connection to Minnesota. (BHL.)

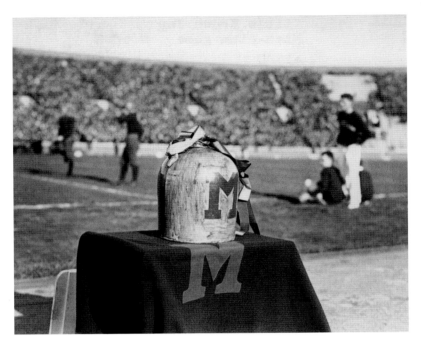

The Little Brown Jug sits proudly on the Michigan sideline during the 1922 game. Michigan retained the jug with a 16-7 victory. (MHS.)

Coach Yost (right) is pictured in 1922 with associates at the Ann Arbor train station after their return from Minneapolis, where Michigan continued its winning streak of three consecutive games over the Gophers. (BHL.)

1910–1933: MICHIGAN TAKES CHARGE

This 1923 game program was the first rendering of the new appearance of the Little Brown Jug. It became the figurehead of all rivalry trophies to come. The two teams were unbeaten in this final game of the season, and Michigan had not lost in three years. Led by All-American team captain Harry Kipke, the Wolverines shut out the Gophers 10-0 in front of a homecoming crowd at Ferry Field. After the season, Coach Yost announced that he would continue with only the full-time responsibilities of the athletic director position. He appointed George Little as Michigan's head coach. (Ken Magee collection.)

The 1924 homecoming magazine *Ski-U-Mah* depicts a player running with the jug. "Ski-U-Mah" was the battle cry for the Gophers created in 1884 by Minnesota rugby captain John Adams after he heard a Sioux Indian canoe-race yell that meant "victory." The Wolverines were again victorious and returned to Ann Arbor with the Little Brown Jug. (Ken Magee collection.)

Bob "Brown

Michigan captain Bob Brown is seen in two photographs from 1925. At left, he proudly displays the results of games while standing in front of Yost Field House. In the image above, he is with a stuffed wolverine on Ferry Field. The Wolverines were victorious over the Gophers, 35-0, in a game where Michigan fielded five All-Americans. Fielding Yost, who had returned to coach the Wolverines that season, called it his greatest team ever despite having lost to Northwestern 3-2 under severe weather conditions earlier in the season. (Both, BHL.)

1910–1933: MICHIGAN TAKES CHARGE

All-American Bennie Oosterbaan stretches for a high pass from fellow All-American and team captain Benny Friedman against Minnesota. In 1926, the two teams played twice: the first game in Ann Arbor, Michigan won handily, 20-0; in the second matchup, the Wolverines defeated the Gophers 7-6 in front of a sold-out crowd of 55,000 fans in Minneapolis. Oosterbaan ran a recovered fumble for a touchdown late in the contest in Minneapolis. Friedman kicked the winning extra point in his last game. In addition, this was the last game Yost ever coached at Michigan. (*Michiganensian* yearbook.)

Bennie Oosterbaan, a three-time All-American, is considered one of the greatest football players of all time and was voted to the first 100 years of college football all-time football team as an end in 1969 by the NCAA. He went on to become head coach from 1948 through 1958 at Michigan. His No. 47 was retired by the University of Michigan. He was elected to the College Football Hall of Fame in 1954. (BHL.)

Benny Friedman leaps high in the air to intercept a Minnesota pass during the 1926 game in Minneapolis. (*Michiganensian* yearbook.)

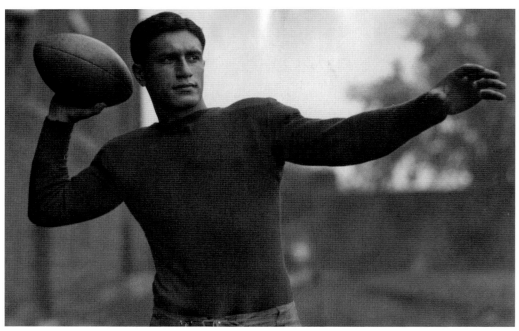

Benny Friedman is part of a legendary passing combination created by Coach Yost where the phrase "Benny to Bennie" (Oosterbaan) became legendary. Friedman was a two-time All-American and team captain for the Wolverines in 1926. He later went on to have a brilliant career in professional football and was an All-Pro quarterback. He was elected to the College Football Hall of Fame in 1954 and Pro Football Hall of Fame in 2005. (BHL.)

1910–1933: MICHIGAN TAKES CHARGE

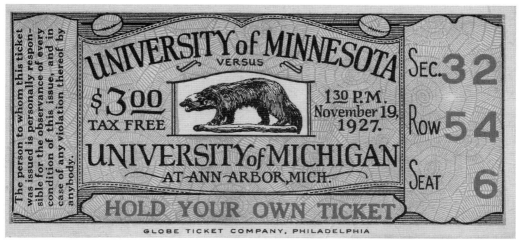

This is the ticket stub to the 1927 game in Ann Arbor, where the Gophers defeated the Wolverines 13-7 in the inaugural season of the newly constructed Michigan Stadium in front of a sold-out homecoming crowd of 84,423. Despite a valiant effort against a superior Gopher team, first-year coach Tad Wieman and team captain Bennie Oosterbaan, who scored a touchdown in his final game, could not stop the Gophers. Minnesota returned to its campus with the Little Brown Jug for the first time since 1919. This was the second time Minnesota won the jug outright since the rivalry began. (Ken Magee collection.)

Herb Joesting was a two-time All-American fullback for the Gophers in 1926 and 1927. He was known as the "Owatonna Thunderbolt." He scored a touchdown in the 1927 Minnesota victory against Michigan. He was elected to the College Football Hall of Fame in 1954. (UMA.)

Ken Haycraft, a 1928 All-American end for Minnesota, scored a touchdown in the 1927 game. He had a brief stint in professional football and was a part of the 1930 NFL champion Green Bay Packers. (UMA.)

Headlines from the *Michigan Daily*, dated November 19, 1927, announce the Minnesota victory over the Wolverines. (BHL.)

1910–1933: MICHIGAN TAKES CHARGE

University of Minnesota co-eds prepare for the 1929 homecoming celebration. Note the pin-back button with small replicas of the Little Brown Jug attached to their lapels. (MHS.)

Homecoming pin-back buttons, such as this 1929 homecoming button for the University of Minnesota, were a celebrated part of the homecoming tradition for the Gophers. They were established in 1914 and continue to this day. Often decorated with symbols of that year's game, they are highly collectable, sought-after items. (Ken Magee collection.)

Bronislau "Bronko" Nagurski's name is synonymous with college football when the discussion of the game's greatest players is the topic. He played many different positions on the field. The 1929 All-American played end and tackle against Michigan in Minnesota's 1927 victory. In 1929, he played at fullback and tackle when the Wolverines shocked the football world by defeating Nagurski and the Gophers 7-6 in front of a sold-out homecoming crowd in Minneapolis. He was inducted into to the College Football Hall of Fame in 1951 and also became a member of the Pro Football Hall of Fame in 1963. His No. 72 was retired by the University of Minnesota in 1979. (UMA.)

This headline from the *Michigan Daily* dated November 17, 1929, followed the 7-6 upset victory by Michigan over the mighty Gophers. (BHL.)

Head coach Fritz Crisler of the Minnesota Gophers arrived on campus in 1930. He coached the Gophers for two seasons before moving to Princeton. Crisler ultimately found his way to the Ann Arbor campus in 1938, where he became a coaching legend and athletic director. His name became synonymous with University of Michigan athletics. (UMA.)

Coach Harry Kipke (white shirt) of the Michigan Wolverines was head coach from 1929 through 1937. He was a former All-American at Michigan in 1922. As head coach, he led the Wolverines to two national titles in 1932 and 1933. (BHL.)

This ticket stub is from the 1930 game in Ann Arbor when the Wolverines defeated the Gophers and first-year head coach Fritz Crisler 7-0. The lone touchdown came after a Clarence "Biggie" Munn punt from Minnesota's own end zone. Michigan's Jack Wheeler returned the punt, dodging, twisting, and turning for 48 yards before finding his way into the Gopher end zone for the game's only score. (Ken Magee collection.)

Clarence "Biggie" Munn was a 1931 All-American at Minnesota as well as Big Ten Conference Most Valuable Player at the guard position. Munn later became head coach at Michigan State University, where his Spartans won the national championship in 1952. He finished his career with Michigan State as the athletic director. He was elected to the College Football Hall of Fame as a coach in 1959. (UMA.)

Gas station attendant K.D. Smith holds what was believed at first to be the official Little Brown Jug that was mysteriously found in a clump of bushes at the Tuomy Hills gas service station at the corner of Washtenaw Avenue and Stadium Boulevard on November 19, 1931, in Ann Arbor (currently the site of the Bearclaw Coffee Company). Earlier in the fall, the Little Brown Jug had been reported stolen from the administration building on Michigan's campus. It was another two years before the official Little Brown Jug was recovered. (*Michiganensian* yearbook.)

Pictured is a ticket to the 1931 homecoming game in Ann Arbor in which the Wolverines won another close game, 6-0. Due to the Depression, in 1931 a sparse crowd of only 37,251 witnessed Michigan's Bill Hewitt bolt 57 yards for the game's only touchdown. (Ken Magee collection.)

Bernie Bierman arrived at Minnesota in 1932. He is seen here (fourth from right) with his players, including his star halfback, two-time All-American Francis "Pug" Lund (third from left). History proved that Coach Bierman, known as the "Grey Eagle," would become one of college football's greatest coaches by winning three straight national championships for Minnesota (1934 to 1936) and five national championships overall. Coach Bierman eventually brought the jug back to Minnesota, where it remained for nine consecutive years. Bierman was inducted into the College Football Hall of Fame in 1955 and Lund was inducted in 1958. (UMA.)

This ticket stub is from the 1932 game in Minneapolis, where the Wolverines defeated the Gophers 3-0. Harry Newman kicked the winning field goal near the end of the first half. A total of 24,766 freezing spectators watched as Michigan secured its first of two consecutive national championships by defeating the Gophers in the final game of the season. (Ken Magee collection.)

Michigan quarterback Harry Newman guided the Wolverines to a national championship in 1932. He was named All-American and was the Douglas Fairbanks Trophy winner, which was the predecessor to the Heisman Trophy as the country's top college football player. He was inducted into the College Football Hall of Fame in 1975. (BHL.)

Michigan's 1932 undefeated national championship squad was led by coach Harry Kipke and All-Americans Chuck Bernard and Harry Newman. The team outscored its opponents 123-13 and recorded six shutouts for the season. (Ken Magee collection.)

The mystery of the stolen Little Brown Jug appears to be solved as Coach Yost displays two jugs. The original, reported as stolen in 1931, was found in the bushes near the University of Michigan Hospital on August 21, 1933. Yost declared that this was the original Little Brown Jug, which it was, effectively admitting that he tried to pass off the jug found at the station two years earlier as the original. Pictured from left to right are Fielding Yost, Wally Weber, Bennie Oosterbaan, Jack Blott, Frank Cappon, and head coach Harry Kipke. (BHL.)

Michigan head coach Harry Kipke entered the 1933 football season as the defending national champion and ended the season again as national champion; however, his 20-game winning streak was disrupted in a battle with the Gophers in late November that ended in a 0-0 tie. (BHL.)

Wolverine center and two-time All-American Chuck Bernard was a key component of Michigan's two consecutive national championship teams. Bernard was called the greatest player in the country by professional coaches in 1933. An outstanding player on both offense and defense, Associated Press sports editor Alan Gould stated, "Without Bernard, the Wolverines could hardly have topped the toughest league in the country." Legend has it that a rally cry for the Gophers was "Stop Bernard." The strategy was not effective, as Bernard never lost to Minnesota, and the Little Brown Jug stayed in Ann Arbor during Bernard's entire career. (BHL.)

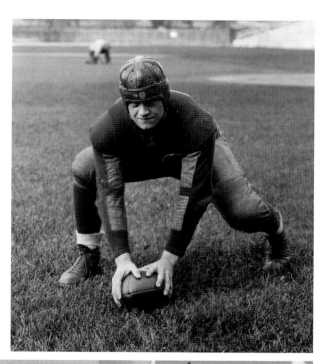

Minnesota
VERSUS
MICHIGAN
AT
ANN ARBOR
SAT. NOV. 18, 1933
2 P. M. E. T.

Est. Price . . $2.50
Tax Paid . . .25
Total $2.75

HOLD YOUR OWN TICKET

SEC. 26 ROW 22 SEAT 16

Shown is a 1933 ticket stub to the contest in Ann Arbor that was played in front of 51,137 fans at Michigan stadium. They witnessed the two teams battle to a scoreless tie. The Wolverines never drove past the Gophers 24-yard line, and even though Minnesota's last-minute field goal attempt was wide, the result caused the only blemish on Michigan's national championship–winning season that ended at 7-0-1. From 1930 through 1933, Michigan posted 25 shutouts and a magnificent 31-1-3 record. (Ken Magee collection.)

Michigan equipment manager Henry Hatch (left) poses on the sidelines of the 1933 Little Brown Jug game. Pictured with Hatch is Michigan cheerleader Joseph Horak. On the 1933 Michigan cheerleading team was a student named Tom Roberts Jr., who was the son of former student manager Tommy Roberts, the original purchaser of the Little Brown Jug in 1903. (BHL.)

Michigan All-American Willie Heston returned to Michigan Stadium for the 30-year anniversary of the historic game in 1903. Maybe it was more than just coincidence that the games in 1903 and in 1933 were both played to a tie. Also, in each of these two seasons, the Wolverines were declared national champions. (BHL.)

4

1934–1942

MINNESOTA DOMINATES

The span of time from 1934 through 1942 saw the most dominating period in the history of the University of Minnesota football program. Upon the arrival of coach Bernie Bierman in Minneapolis in 1932, he quickly turned the Gophers into a powerhouse football machine and won his first national championship in 1934. The Gophers did not slow down after defeating Michigan that year. Including the 1934 victory, Minnesota reeled off nine consecutive victories against Michigan, giving the Little Brown Jug permanent residence in Minnesota for a lengthy time.

The nine-game winning streak is a feat never accomplished against Michigan by any other college football program. To put this streak in perspective, Heisman Trophy–winner Tom Harmon's overall career record while playing at Michigan was 19-4-1; of the four losses, three were against Minnesota. Tom Harmon never won the Little Brown Jug in his career, a regret he carried throughout his life.

The 1934 Minnesota dynasty continued to rule the football world through 1936, winning a third consecutive national championship. Minnesota brought Bierman his fourth national championship in 1940, which was preserved by Bruce Smith's 80-yard touchdown run in Minnesota's 7-6 victory over Michigan. In 1941, Smith won the Heisman Trophy, and the Gophers won another national championship. During Coach Bierman's tenure at Minnesota, he won five national championships and seven Big Ten Conference championships from 1932 to 1941 at Minnesota.

This is the 1934 game program and ticket stub for the game in Minneapolis. The Wolverines traveled to Minneapolis to play the mighty Gophers during their homecoming weekend. The Gophers did not disappoint their fans and soundly defeated the Wolverines 34-0. It was the first time in 42 years that Minnesota had defeated Michigan in Minneapolis. This game set the stage for years to come, as the Gophers dominated Michigan for the next nine years straight. Also during this era, Minnesota dominated the nation, winning three consecutive national championships and five overall. (Both, Ken Magee collection.)

Francis "Pug" Lund was the greatest player he ever coached according to legendary coach Bernie Bierman. Lund was a walk-on quarterback from Rice Lake, Wisconsin. As the Gopher left halfback, he helped Minnesota demolish Michigan in 1934 and was showered with national honors that year. He was a two-time All-American in 1933 and 1934, as well as the Big Ten Conference Most Valuable Player in 1934. He was inducted into the College Football Hall of Fame in 1958. (UMA.)

Frank "Butch" Larson, Minnesota's end, earned All-American status in 1933 and 1934. He was a key player on Bernie Bierman's 1934 national championship team. (UMA.)

Pictured are Fielding Yost (left), 1934 Wolverine captain Tom Austin, and Coach Kipke. Austin had the misfortune of being the captain for a Michigan team that suffered one of the worst season records in Michigan football history: an overall 1-7 record with 0-6 mark in the Big Ten Conference. (Ken Magee collection.)

Michigan center Gerald "Jerry" Ford, a native of Grand Rapids, Michigan, played center for the Wolverines from 1932 to 1934. In his first two years of eligibility, his playing time was limited, as he was backup to two-time All-American Chuck Bernard. He was voted the 1934 team most valuable player in his final year. After his playing days at Michigan, he went to law school at Yale and eventually entered a career in politics. He became the 38th president of the United States in 1974. Gerald R. Ford had his No. 48 football jersey retired by the University of Michigan in 1994. (BHL.)

Michigan is pictured on defense during the 1934 Minnesota game in Minneapolis. As hard as the Wolverines tried, including holding the Gophers to a scoreless first half, Minnesota's skill and power broke the Wolverine defense as they out-rushed Michigan 314 to 17 yards and scored five consecutive second-half touchdowns in a 34-0 rout. (*Michiganensian* yearbook.)

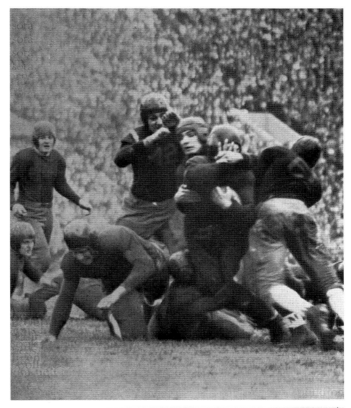

Pug Lund holds the Little Brown Jug along with Coach Bierman and former 1903 Gopher standout quarterback Sig Harris after the 1934 homecoming game victory. (UMA.)

Oscar Munson paints the game score on the Little Brown Jug after the 1934 Minnesota victory. (UMA.)

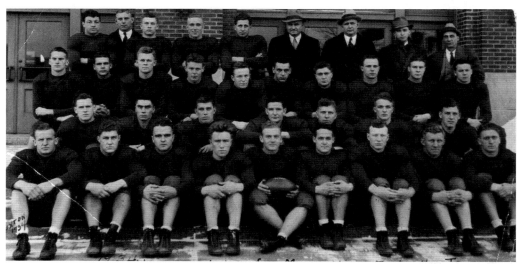

This photograph shows Minnesota's 1934 national championship team. The Gophers were an undefeated 8-0 for the season and outscored their opponents 270-38, becoming the first of several Bernie Bierman teams to win the national championship. (UMA.)

Oscar Munson secures the Little Brown Jug during the 1935 matchup in Ann Arbor. A total of 32,029 spectators watched as the Gophers handed Michigan its second consecutive loss and shutout by trouncing the Wolverines 40-0. (UMA.)

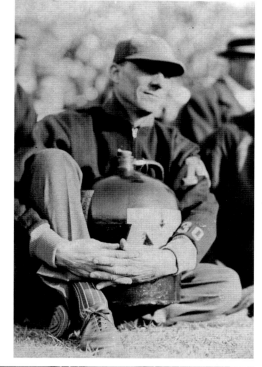

Here is Minnesota's 1935 national championship team. It was a second consecutive national title for Coach Bierman, as his team went an undefeated 8-0 and extended its total undefeated streak to 24 consecutive games. (UMA.)

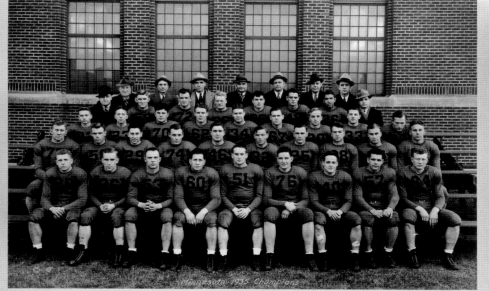

Minnesota 1935 Champions

Sig Harris; Oscar Munson; Dr. Geo Hauser; Bernie Bierman; Frank McCormick; Bert Baston; Lowell Dawson

Lloyd Stein, trainer; Ed Kafka; Russ Wile; Harvey Ring; Victor Spadaccini; Ray King; Dwight Reed; Clark Snyder, mgr.

Sam Hunt; William Matheny; Louis Midler; Charles Wilkinson; Ray Antil; Whitman Rork; Rudolph Gmitro; Frank Warner; Bob Weld

Edwin Widseth; Earl Svendsen; Clarence Thompson; Ray Trampe; B.Willis Smith; Andrew Uram; Malcolm Eiken; Sam Riley; Stanley Hanson; Dominic Klesowski

Geo Rennix; Vernal LeVoir; Frank Dallers; Sheldon Beise; Glenn Seidel, Capt; Richard Smith; Dale Rennebohm; Geo Roscoe; Vern Oech

Ed Widseth, a two-time All-American tackle in 1935 and 1936 for the Gophers, was part of the famous front line of Minnesota known as the "Seven Blocks of Granite." After college, he entered professional football and was the NFL Player of the Year for the New York Giants in 1938. He was inducted into the College Football Hall of Fame in 1954. (UMA.)

Charles "Bud" Wilkinson was an incredible athlete from south Minneapolis. He was an All-American guard in 1935. He switched positions in 1936 and became the Gopher quarterback. Running the offense, he led Minnesota to its third consecutive national championship. He was quite the athlete, as he was also an outstanding goalie for the Gopher hockey team. After his playing days, he became the head coach of the University of Oklahoma, where he won three national championships. His Sooners also hold the record for the longest winning streak in college football history by winning 47 consecutive games. He was inducted into the College Football Hall of Fame as a coach in 1969. (UMA.)

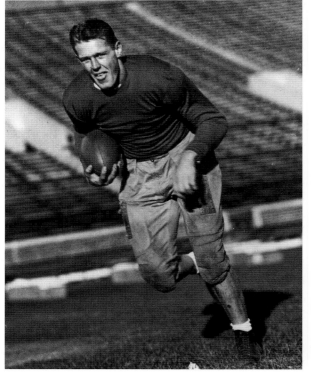

Minnesota's 1936 team won a third consecutive national championship for Coach Bierman. The Gophers compiled a 7-1 record, losing only to Northwestern when the Wildcats shut them out 6-0. Minnesota only surrendered 32 points the entire season. (UMA.)

A photograph from 1936 depicts a huge replica of the Little Brown Jug. This extremely rare Red Wing, 15-gallon jug, known as the "Directors Jug," was utilized as an advertising piece and was placed in the window of the Red Wing Pottery Store located at 2345 University Avenue in Saint Paul, Minnesota, the current site of Twin City Janitor Supply. The Directors Jug was owned by longtime Red Wing Pottery employee and collector Stan Bougie, and in the late 1970s it was sold to fellow Red Wing pottery collector Mark Cellotti. (MHS.)

Co-eds are pictured on the Minnesota campus with a large supply of homecoming pin-back buttons for the 1938 celebration. The campus had a lot to celebrate, as the Gophers secured possession of the Little Brown Jug that year. (Above, MHS; at left, Ken Magee collection.)

Michigan's Tom Harmon played from 1938 to 1940 and was considered one of the legends of the game. A two-time All-American in 1939 and 1940, he also won the Heisman Trophy in 1940. His No. 98 was retired by Michigan in 1940. Harmon was often quoted as saying that his biggest disappointment was never winning the Little Brown Jug, as his teams were a combined 0-3 against the Gophers. Harmon took sole responsibility for Michigan's 1938 and 1940 losses to the Gophers. In 1938, his fumble led to a Gopher touchdown, and in 1940 his extra-point kick went wide. The Gophers defeated the Wolverines both years by the identical score of 7-6. He was inducted into the College Football Hall of Fame in 1954. (BHL.)

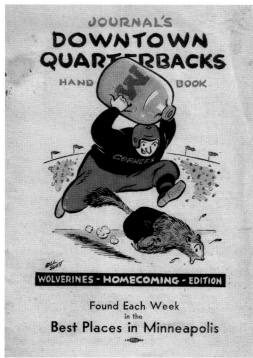

The image on the front of this 1938 "Downtown Quarterbacks" handbook proved to be prophetic, as the Gophers defeated the Wolverines 7-6 in front of a Minneapolis homecoming crowd of 54,212 fans at Memorial Stadium. This loss spoiled first-year Michigan coach Fritz Crisler's debut against his former team. The Gophers went on to win their fourth Big Ten Conference championship in the last five years. (Ken Magee collection.)

A souvenir menu from the 1938 banquet sponsored in Minneapolis depicts the 1938 Wolverines team and Coach Crisler with captain Fred Janke (also seen is Janke's autograph). (Ken Magee collection.)

The Brown Jug Restaurant is located at 1204 South University in Ann Arbor and was established in 1938. It was named in honor of the historic series between Michigan and Minnesota and pays homage to the Little Brown Jug. This popular eatery for students still exists in the heart of the University of Michigan's main campus. The Brown Jug is currently owned by Perry Porikos, who told the authors a story about the days in his youth when he was a dishwasher there. He promised his friends back then that one day he would be the owner of the restaurant. Many years later, Perry kept his promise. (Jon Stevens collection.)

The 1939 game played in Ann Arbor saw the Gophers again soundly defeat the Wolverines 20-7 in front of 66,572 spectators at Michigan Stadium. Minnesota's sixth consecutive victory over the Wolverines earned the Gophers the opportunity to again return to Minneapolis with the Little Brown Jug. (Ken Magee collection.)

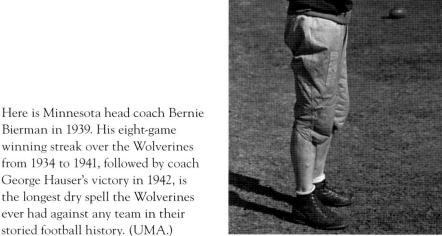

Here is Minnesota head coach Bernie Bierman in 1939. His eight-game winning streak over the Wolverines from 1934 to 1941, followed by coach George Hauser's victory in 1942, is the longest dry spell the Wolverines ever had against any team in their storied football history. (UMA.)

Michigan fullback Bob Westfall (No. 86) carries the football during the 1939 matchup. Tom Harmon (No. 98) prepares to block for his teammate. This was the second year that the Wolverines would wear the now-famous "winged" helmet, brought to Michigan by Fritz Crisler from Princeton. This allowed the quarterback to spot the receivers clearly when they were downfield. (*Michiganensian* yearbook.)

Future Heisman Trophy–winner Bruce Smith dives across the goal line in 1939 to score the Gophers' third and final touchdown in their 20-7 victory. (*Michiganensian* yearbook.)

Shown here is the 1940 official game program for what has been considered arguably the most famous game in the series, as the top two teams in the nation battled it out on a wet and muddy Memorial Stadium field. The game featured two Heisman Trophy winners, Tom Harmon (1940) and Bruce Smith (1941). It was fitting that both Harmon and Smith accounted for the game's only touchdowns. Harmon passed to captain Forest Evashevski for a Michigan touchdown and Harmon's attempt at the extra point failed. Smith then electrified the crowd with an 80-yard run to tie the game. Joe Mernik's extra point was good, sealing the victory for the Gophers. Minnesota won its fifth conference championship that year and fourth national title in the last seven years. (Ken Magee collection.)

UNIVERSITY OF MINNESOTA
OFFICIAL FOOTBALL PROGRAM

Michigan vs. Minnesota

Saturday, November 9, 1940

OFFICIALS FOR TODAY'S GAME

Referee: Frank Birch (Earlham)   Field Judge: Jack Crangle (Illinois)
Umpire: W. D. Knight (Dartmouth)   Linesman: Don Hamilton (Notre Dame)

THE PLAYERS

Minnesota					Michigan			
No.	Name	Exp.	Position	Weight	No.	Name	Position	Weight
16	Van Sistine, Leo	1	End	185	7	Manalakas, George	Halfback	160
19	Shearer, Jim*	2	Quarterback	177	10	Day, Frank	Halfback	165
20	Kolander, Jerry	1	Halfback	167	11	Wistert, Albert	Tackle	212
22	Geelan, George	1	Back	170	19	Denise, Theodore	Guard	187
23	Lundeen, Ralph	1	End	175	22	Melzow, William	Guard	185
24	Mernik, Joe*	2	Halfback	176	23	Nelson, David	Halfback	165
30	Kolliner, Bob*	3	Center	176	27	Laine, John	Guard	185
33	Paffrath, Bob*	3	QB-HB	186	28	Zimmerman, Robert	Fullback	180
34	Hirscher, Joe	2	End	187	33	Kennedy, Ted	Center	185
35	Bartelt, John*	2	Quarterback	188	36	Cunningham, Leo	Guard	188
37	Franck, George*	3	Halfback	175	38	Smeja, Rudy	End	200
38	Flick, Gene	2	Center	189	39	Karwales, John	End	180
40	Garnaas, Bill	1	Halfback	174	40	Woytek, Louis	Center	170
41	Ring, Rolland	1	HB-QB	168	42	Lockard, Harold	Halfback	180
42	Lund, Bert	1	Quarterback	182	43	Smith, Robert B.	Tackle	210
43	Straiton, Howard	1	Guard	188	45	Anderson, Harry	Center	210
45	Daley, Bill	1	Fullback	200	48	Butler, Jack	Tackle	193
46	Solheim, Bob	1	Center	195	49	Hall, Clarence	End	192
47	Fitch, Bob*	2	End	201	54	Grissen, James	Fullback	185
48	Paschka, Gordon*	2	Guard	206	55	Call, Norman	Halfback	170
49	Jamnik, Joe*	3	Halfback	183	56	Sengel, Rudolph	Tackle	217
50	Johnson, Bill*	3	End	195	57	Sharpe, Phillip	End	185
	(Co-captain)				58	Kelto, Reuben	Tackle	195
51	Bicanich, John	1	Guard	202	59	Sukup, Milo	Guard	190
52	Evans, Woodrow	1	End	189	60	Wise, Clifford	Halfback	170
53	Billman, John*	2	Guard	192	63	Fritz, Ralph	Guard	202
54	Smith, Bruce*	2	Halfback	193	64	Madar, Elmer	Halfback	180
55	Steinbauer, Ed*	3	Fullback	195	66	Ingalls, Robert	Center	200
56	Newell, Jerry	1	Back	185	68	Fraumann, Harlin	End	190
57	Johnson, Vic	1	Tackle	201	69	Evashevski, Forest	Quarterback	198
58	Bierhaus, Gene	1	Quarterback	179	70	Seltzer, Holbrooke	Guard	165
59	Berthon, Tom	1	Guard	194	71	Megregian, Michael	Quarterback	180
60	Nolander, Don	1	Center	201	73	Flora, Robert	Tackle	215
62	Saunders, Bob	1	Guard	194	76	Gannatal, Paul	Halfback	185
63	Holmstrom, Wallace	1	Guard	210	78	Rogers, Joe	End	200
64	Kuusisto, Bill*	3	Guard	222	80	Krejsa, Robert	Halfback	190
65	Vant Hull, Fred*	2	Tackle	209	82	Hildebrandt, George	Guard	185
67	Ekberg, Carl	1	End	201	83	Kromer, Paul	Halfback	165
68	Sweiger, Bob*	2	Fullback	206	84	Czak, Edward	End	180
69	Nelson, Bernie	1	Center	194	86	Westfall, Bob	Fullback	175
70	Ringer, Judd	2	End	194	87	Frutig, Edward	End	180
71	Brody, Bob	1	Halfback	186	88	Kohl, Harry	Halfback	150
72	Plunkett, Warren	1	FB-QB	194	89	Ciethaml, George	Quarterback	190
73	Welch, Mike	1	QB-FB	195	96	Kolesar, Robert	Guard	198
74	Odson, Urban*	2	Tackle	247	98	Harmon, Tom	Halfback	195
75	Mitchell, Paul	1	Tackle	205				
76	Levy, Leonard*	2	Tackle	226				
77	Pukema, Helge	3	Guard	201				
78	Bjorklund, Bob*	3	C-E	219				
	(Co-captain)					University of Michigan—Ann Arbor,		
79	Lushine, Jim	1	Tackle	234		Michigan		
80	Townley, John	1	Tackle	221				
81	O'Bradovich, Mike	1	Halfback	181				
82	Anderson, Cliff	1	End	185		Team Nickname—Wolverines		
83	Emerson, Conrad	1	Tackle	191				
85	Moore, Mark	2	Center	189				
86	Lechner, Ed	2	Tackle	200		Coach—Herbert (Fritz) Crisler,		
87	Baumgartner, Bill	1	End	183		Chicago, 3rd year		
88	Gladwin, Bill	2	End	183				
89	Riley, Tom	2	Guard	185				
90	Litman, Neil*	2	Guard	216		Score last season—Minn. 20, Mich. 7		
94	Wildung, Dick	1	Tackle	210				
95	Lauterbach, Joe	1	Quarterback	199				
97	Smith, Bob*	2	Guard	199				

* Denotes Lettermen

TO OUR PATRONS:
The use of intoxicating liquors in this Stadium is prohibited. Ushers and officers have been instructed to refuse admission to holders of tickets who are intoxicated. We shall revoke the license conferred by the ticket and eject from the Stadium anyone violating this restriction.

FRANK G. McCORMICK, Director of Athletics

OVER

MICHIGAN
VERSUS
MINNESOTA

SATURDAY, NOVEMBER 9, 1940

BENCH SEAT KICKOFF—2:00 P. M.

Est. Price $2.50
Fed. Tax...... .25

Total $2.75

UNIVERSITY of MINNESOTA
MEMORIAL
STADIUM

NO REFUNDS

**ENTER GATE
THAT BEARS
SECTION
NUMBER**

BENCH SEAT
18 5 5
SEAT ROW BENCH
HOLD YOUR OWN TICKET
RETAIN THIS CHECK
BENCH SEAT

Est. Price $2.50—Fed. Tax 25c—Total $2.75
MICHIGAN vs. MINNESOTA
Sat. Nov. 9, 1940
BENCH SEAT
18 5 5
BENCH ROW SEAT

This ticket is from the 1940 game between Michigan and Minnesota at Memorial Stadium. The game was played in front of 60,481 spectators. The result was a Minnesota victory, 7-6. It was Minnesota's seventh consecutive victory over the Wolverines, and the Little Brown Jug remained in Minneapolis. (Ken Magee collection.)

GEORGE FRANCK, All-American Halfback
Winner of the 1940 Outstanding Athlete in Minneapolis
Award by the Minneapolis Junior Association of Commerce.
January 9, 1941   Minneapolis, Minnesota

A commemorative card depicts George "Sonny" Franck, an All-American for the Gophers in 1940 who also came in third place for the Heisman Trophy. He was a world-class sprinter and captain of the Gopher track team. He used that speed to beat opponents on the gridiron. In the 1941 College All-Star Game, he played in the same backfield with Michigan's Tom Harmon and was voted the game's most valuable player. This card was autographed by Gopher legend John McGovern and Michigan's own Tom Harmon. (LJ.)

A classic photograph depicts two football legends: Tom Harmon with the football being tackled by Minnesota's Bruce Smith in the 1940 battle of the unbeatens. While both Harmon and Smith would win the Heisman Trophy (Harmon in 1940 and Smith in 1941), Smith at Minnesota never lost to Michigan and Harmon never defeated Minnesota. In fact, Harmon never scored a rushing touchdown against Minnesota during his entire college career. (UMA.)

This 1941 ticket stub honors Michigan's already-graduated Tom Harmon after he had won the Heisman Trophy the year before. The game was in Ann Arbor with a homecoming crowd of 84,658. Minnesota shut out the Wolverines 7-0. The loss was Michigan's only defeat of the season and earned the undefeated 8-0 Minnesota Gophers the Big Ten Conference and national championship. Minnesota had now won the Little Brown Jug for eight consecutive years. (Ken Magee collection.)

Minnesota's Bruce Smith, the 1941 Heisman Trophy winner, led the Gophers to two national championships in 1940 and 1941. His father, Lucius Smith, played on the 1910 Gopher team that lost to the Wolverines. Legend has it that Lucius told all who would listen after the 1910 Gopher defeat that he would some day have a son who would play for Minnesota and defeat the Wolverines. Bruce turned out to defeat the Wolverines, not once, but three times in his career. Also, he became an All-American and won the Heisman trophy in 1941. Bruce Smith was inducted into the College Football Hall of Fame in 1972. His No. 54 was retired by the University of Minnesota in 1977. (TB.)

This 1941 game-action photograph highlights the Wolverines and Gophers at Michigan Stadium. Michigan quarterback George Ceithaml (No. 89) has the ball. Also pictured for Michigan are halfback Tom Kuzma (No. 45) and All-American tackle Albert "Ox" Wistert (No. 11). Minnesota's Leonard Levy (No. 76) gives chase in the background. (*Michiganensian* yearbook.)

1934–1942: MINNESOTA DOMINATES

A photograph captures the 1941 Minnesota national championship team. This squad gave Coach Bierman his fifth and final national championship. With a perfect 8-0 season, the mighty Gophers outscored their opponents 186-38. Bierman then entered the armed services. While stationed at the Iowa Pre-Flight Naval Training Center in 1942, he coached the Seahawks to a 26-14 victory over Michigan. With this victory, Coach Bierman accomplished nine consecutive wins over Michigan, equaling the Gophers' same achievement. Coincidentally, in 1942, Michigan finally won (9-0) against former Gopher Bruce Smith, who was playing for the Great Lakes Naval Training Station Bluejackets. (UMA.)

A 1942 *Alumni Weekly* magazine for homecoming shows a jug floating in the Pacific Ocean. At the height of World War II, the battle on the gridiron proved to be intense. A disputed Minnesota field goal on the last play of the first half proved to be the difference. Michigan claimed that the clock had expired, but the play stood as called. At the end of the game, Minnesota was victorious, 16-14. (Ken Magee collection.)

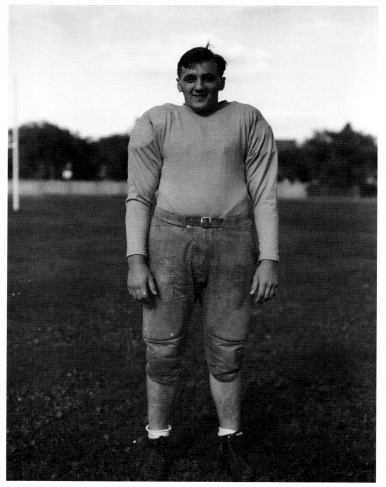

Here is a 1942 game ticket to Memorial Stadium. The Little Brown Jug remained in Minneapolis much to the delight of the 49,181 spectators who saw Minnesota edge the favored Wolverines. This game marked the ninth straight season the Gophers defeated the Wolverines. (Ken Magee collection.)

Tackle and captain Dick Wildung played for Bernie Bierman's two national championship teams in 1940 and 1941. He earned All-American honors in 1941 and 1942. He went on to have a successful professional career with the Green Bay Packers. He was inducted into the College Football Hall of Fame in 1957. (UMA.)

Michigan halfback Tom Kuzma is tackled by a swarm of Minnesota defenders during the 1942 game at Minneapolis, which the Gophers won 16-14. (*Michiganensian* yearbook.)

A classic 1942 photograph shows Coach Crisler (center), captain George Ceithaml (left), and Albert "Ox" Wistert in the practice area of Ferry Field in Ann Arbor. (BHL.)

Oscar Munson poses with the Little Brown Jug in Minneapolis in 1942. This was the last year Minnesota would possess the real jug before losing it for the next 10 years. (UMA.)

Oscar Munson is seen "guarding" a replica of the Little Brown Jug. Although this is a great publicity photograph, historians ("jugologists") believe it is a replica jug based on three facts: the block M appears to be elongated, the issue of Nature Magazine is dated October 1948, and Minnesota had a dry spell during that era, not winning the jug from 1943 to 1952. (MHS.)

5

1 9 4 3 – 1 9 6 8
THE BATTLE CONTINUES

World War II had a significant impact on various football programs. In 1943, servicemen transfers resulted in many star football players moving from student status at their prior year's respective university to military training programs at other designated universities. In the Big Ten Conference, schools that benefited from these student-servicemen transfers were Michigan, Northwestern, and Purdue. Other schools that were significantly depleted of their football talent were Minnesota, Wisconsin, and Illinois. This shifted the balance of football power from Minnesota to Michigan in the battle for the Little Brown Jug.

Beginning in 1943, Michigan won the Little Brown Jug 10 consecutive times. It was also during this period that Coach Fritz Crisler led the Wolverines to a national championship in 1947. The talent at Michigan was superb, and the following year newly appointed Coach Bennie Oosterbaan guided his Wolverines to their second consecutive national championship. Both Crisler and Oosterbaan were awarded unprecedented back-to-back National Coach of the Year awards for their success on the gridiron.

As the rivalry continued into the 1950s and 1960s, the teams were almost evenly matched in the battle for the Little Brown Jug. Minnesota returned to national prominence under the leadership of coach Murray Warmath, who became National Coach of the Year by leading his Minnesota Gophers to the national championship in 1960. The end of the 1960s led to another major change in the Little Brown Jug rivalry's balance of power with the arrival of coach Bo Schembechler at Michigan.

This is a 1943 ticket stub to the Little Brown Jug contest held in Ann Arbor in front of a "sparse" homecoming crowd of 42,966. The Wolverines finally got the upper hand on the Gophers, after nine consecutive losses, by trouncing them 49-6. Michigan halfback Elroy "Crazy Legs" Hirsch ran 61 yards for a touchdown on the first play of the game, and Michigan never looked back. Hirsch scored two more touchdowns and Michigan's fullback Bill Daley tallied two more touchdowns. (Ken Magee collection.)

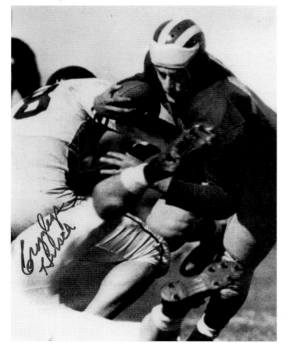

Michigan halfback "Crazy Legs" Hirsch dives for a touchdown in 1943. Hirsch was a 1943 University of Wisconsin serviceman transfer. In this image versus Northwestern, defending halfback Herman Frickey was a University of Minnesota serviceman transfer to the Wildcats. Earlier in 1941, Frickey scored the lone touchdown for the Gophers in a 7-0 win against the Wolverines. Michigan fullback Bill Daley also was a 1943 serviceman transfer from the University of Minnesota and an All-American that year. Hirsch was inducted into the College Football Hall of Fame in 1974. He also was a Los Angeles Rams split end who was inducted into the Pro Football Hall of Fame in 1968. These are examples of the unique servicemen transfers in 1943 that occurred under World War II conditions. (MS.)

Bill Daley was the first player to win the Little Brown Jug four consecutive times; however, this feat will most likely never be done again in the way Daley achieved it. Daley played three years for the Gophers, from 1940 to 1942, before transferring to a military unit at the University of Michigan, where he played his fourth year for the Wolverines. At Michigan, he earned All-American status in 1943. He was considered a Minnesota hero by intercepting two passes against the Wolverines in the 1941 game. After playing on two national championship teams at Minnesota, Daley was determined to win the jug for Michigan against his former teammates as demonstrated in this inscribed photograph to Henry Hatch, Michigan's equipment manager. Daley's determination paid off, as his Wolverines defeated the Gophers 49-6. (At right, UMA; below, BHL.)

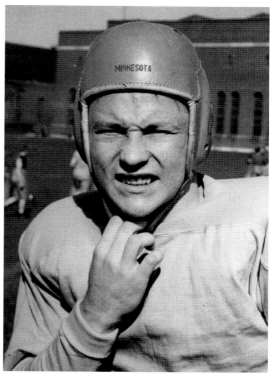

To Honk,
Best Wishes, and lets hope michigan wins This Jug. Sincerly Bill Daley

A presentation of an honorary souvenir jug was made in 1944 to the original Michigan purchaser of the Little Brown Jug in 1903, former student manager Tommy Roberts (far right). Roberts later memorialized his role in the historical battle by penning a poem: "These are the simple facts of the case / and I guess I ought to know / They say that Oscar 'discovered' the jug / and I'm not denying it so / The years have deprived me of most of my hair / the little that's left is grey / but I'm the guy that PURCHASED the jug / and they'll never take that away." (Ken Magee collection.)

This photograph shows the 1947 offensive unit for the University of Michigan. The Wolverines were favorites to defeat the Gophers and keep the Little Brown Jug. Minnesota held tough before losing 13-6 in front of a Michigan homecoming crowd of 85,938. All-Americans Bob Chappuis and Chalmers "Bump" Elliott connected on a go-ahead 40-yard touchdown pass. The 10-0 squad won the Big Ten Conference and national championship after a Rose Bowl 49-0 victory. Chappuis came in second for the Heisman Trophy. He was inducted into the College Football Hall of Fame in 1988. Elliott was inducted in 1989. (Ken Magee collection.)

1943–1968: THE BATTLE CONTINUES

Welcome to Another Homecoming

ALUMNI

Here's one weekend that's all yours. Even though you don't recognize all the new faces, you know we all have something in common . . . the Spirit of Michigan!

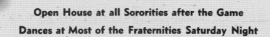

Highlights on Campus this Weekend

Saturday

SPORTS:
Annual "Little Brown Jug" Game between SAE's and Phi Delts. 10:00 A.M. at corner of South University and Washtenaw.
Michigan-Minnesota Game. Kickoff at 2 P.M.

DANCING:
Homecoming Dance at the Intramural Building, beginning at 8:30 P.M.
Michigan Union Dance beginning at 9:00 P.M.
Dance at the Michigan League Ballroom, 9:00 to 12:00 P.M.
Masonic Temple Dance, from 9:00 P.M. to 1:00 A.M.

MOVIES:
Lydia Mendelssohn Theatre: "I Live As I Please" at 8:30 P.M. (Italian Film with English Subtitles).
Michigan Theatre: "Variety Girl" (Hope, Crosby, & Co.)
State Theatre: "Brute Force" (Burt Lancaster).

Sunday

MUSIC:
Recordings of Classics. Michigan League, second floor from 4:00 P.M. to 6:00 P.M.
Hot Record Society. Michigan League at 8:00 P.M.
University Carillonneur 3:00 P.M. and at 7:15 P.M.

EXHIBITS:
Alumni Memorial Hall: "Modern Handmade Jewelry" and "Fine Arts under Fire." Open from 2:00 to 5:00 P.M.
The Museum of Archeology, open from 3:00 to 5:00 P.M.
University Museum, open from 2:00-5:00 P.M. (Owosso dinosaur now on display).

Open House at all Sororities after the Game

Dances at Most of the Fraternities Saturday Night

Here Are the Ann Arbor Merchants Who Sponsored this Page

REMEMBER THEM?

RABIDEAU-HARRIS 119 South Main	**OVERBECK BOOKSTORE** 1216 South University	**DICK'S RECORD SHOP** 1114 South University	**WHITE SPOT RESTAURANT** 517 East William
BROOKINS SHOE STORE 108 East Washington	**THE DILLON SHOP** 309 South State	**SAFFELL & BUSH** 310 South State	**JACOBSON'S** 612 East Liberty
AL O'GRADY'S BARBER SHOP 1110 South University	**RAMSAY-CANFIELD, INC.** 119 East Liberty	**SLATER'S BOOK STORE, INC.** 336 South State	**CALKINS-FLETCHER DRUG CO.** 324 South State
STOLL BICYCLE SHOP 424 South Main	**TEMPLE CAFETERIA** 327 South Fourth Avenue	**AVON BEAUTY SHOP** 234 Nickels Arcade	**Wahr's University Book Store** 316 South State
MORRILL'S 314 South State	**Follett's Michigan Book Store** 322 South State	**ULRICH'S BOOK STORE** 549 East University	**MADEMOISELLE, INC.** 302 South State
WILD'S 311 South State	**COON'S LENDING LIBRARY** 14 Nickels Arcade	**VAN BUREN SHOP** 8 Nickels Arcade	**L. G. BALFOUR CO.** 1319 South University
MOE SPORT SHOP 1317 South University	**Ann Arbor Business School** 330 South State	**GRANADA CAFE** 313 South State	**TOWN & CAMPUS SHOES** 1317 South University

Prior to the 1947 homecoming weekend and matchup between the Wolverines and the Gophers, the *Michigan Daily* sold homecoming weekend–related advertisements to various merchants around Ann Arbor. Of the 28 merchants who supported the Wolverines in this full-page advertisement, only one remains in existence. Moe Sport Shops, acquired by Underground Printing, Inc., in 2010, maintains its business address at 711 North University in Ann Arbor. (BHL.)

A giant display stands in front of Michigan's West Quad during the 1947 homecoming weekend. With the Little Brown Jug in tow, the two Michigan characters cheer on the Wolverines to beat the Gophers into the ground. (BHL.)

Two governors, Minnesota's Harold Stassen (left) and Michigan's Kim Sigler, exchange pleasantries over the Little Brown Jug while the Michigan band plays in the background at the 1947 game in Ann Arbor. Stassen was a perennial US presidential candidate, tallying 13 attempts beginning in 1940. (CP.)

Michigan's famous 1947 backfield members were known as the "Mad Magicians" for their intricate ball handling and trick plays on the field. From left to right are Bump Elliott, Howard Yerges, Jack Weisenburger, and Bob Chappuis. (Ken Magee collection.)

Here are headlines for the *Michigan Daily* following the Michigan victory over Minnesota in the 1947 matchup. (BHL.)

The last season that Fritz Crisler coached the Wolverines was 1947; he then began focusing solely on his duties as athletic director at Michigan. His final team went an undefeated 10-0, won the Rose Bowl game 49-0 against the University of Southern California, and was declared the national champion. Crisler was also voted 1947 National Coach of the Year by the Associated Press. His career record at Michigan was 71-16-3, and his winning percentage of .805 ranks him second in school history behind only Fielding Yost in all-time winning percentage. (Ken Magee collection.)

In 1948, a familiar face would lead the Wolverines. Bennie Oosterbaan was appointed football head coach and is seen here with Alvin "Moose" Wistert, one of three great Wistert brothers. Francis, Albert, and Alvin were All-Americans and each wore No. 11, which was retired by Michigan. The Wolverines defeated the Gophers in Minneapolis 27-14 in 1948 and ended the season undefeated at 9-0 and won their second consecutive national championship. All three Wisterts were inducted into the College Football Hall of Fame: Francis in 1967, Albert in 1968, and Alvin in 1981. (BHL.)

Clayton "Two-Ton Tonny" Tonnemaker played center for the Gophers from 1946 to 1949. Selected as an All-American in 1949, he was also a defensive star alongside of Leo Nomellini. The two were credited with holding the mighty 1947 Wolverines to just 22 yards rushing and 73 passing yards. The 1947 contest was a close game, which resulted in a 13-6 Michigan victory. Tonnemaker was inducted into the College Football Hall of Fame in 1980. (UMA.)

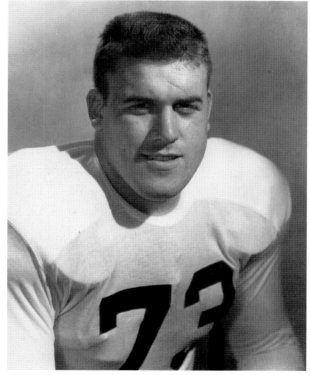

Leo "the Lion" Nomellini, born in Italy and raised in Chicago, was an All-American tackle for the Gophers in 1948 and 1949. Although he and Tonnemaker never defeated the Wolverines, Nomellini ranks as one of the game's all-time greats. He was inducted into the College Football Hall of Fame in 1977 and Pro Football Hall of Fame in 1969. (UMA.)

Bud Grant, a star end at Minnesota, earned nine letters while playing multiple sports for the Gophers from 1946 to 1950. He was selected as Minnesota's "Athlete of the Half Century" and went on to become a coaching legend, taking the Minnesota Vikings to four Super Bowls. He was inducted into the Pro Football Hall of Fame in 1994. (UMA.)

Shown is the 1950 game program for the Little Brown Jug contest fought in Minneapolis. In Bernie Bierman's last year as head coach, the Gophers surprised the Wolverines, and the game ended in a 7-7 tie. Michigan's only score was from fullback Don Dufek. The Gophers' Darrell Cochran scored a touchdown late in the fourth quarter. Michigan ended the season winning its fourth consecutive Big Ten Conference championship and defeating California in the Rose Bowl 14-6. Dufek went on to have two sons who were both All-American football players at Michigan: Don in 1975 and Bill in 1976. (Ken Magee collection.)

MICHIGAN
VS
MINNESOTA

MEMORIAL STADIUM   OCTOBER 28, 1950

The
GOPHER
GOALPOST

OFFICIAL
PROGRAM

25
CENTS

JERRY EKBERG
SENIOR
RIGHT TACKLE

BAND DAY

TEAM LINEUPS ON PAGE 16

Michigan standout linebacker Roger Zatkoff (No. 70) helps tackle a Minnesota ball carrier in the 1952 contest in Ann Arbor. The Wolverines defeated the Gophers 21-0 to win their 10th consecutive Little Brown Jug in a mistake-filled game, where both teams combined for a total of 10 turnovers. (*Michiganensian* yearbook.)

Lowell Perry was an accomplished end and safety for Michigan. He earned All-American honors in 1951. He is seen here catching a pass during the 1952 Minnesota homecoming game played in Ann Arbor in front of 72,404 spectators. He had a Michigan single-game record for receiving yards gained—165—which was not broken until Jack Clancy had 197 yards in 1966. (*Michiganensian* yearbook.)

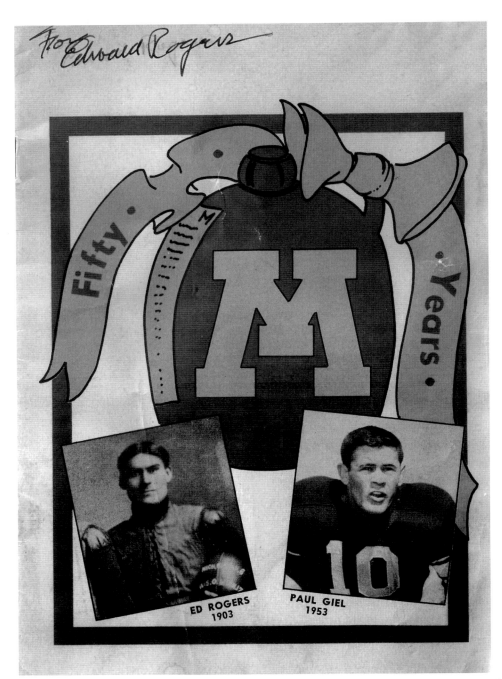

This 50th anniversary banquet program was autographed by 1903 Minnesota captain Ed Rogers. The celebration in Minneapolis for the event was held at the Nicollet Hotel and was well documented. It was attended by many of the players and coaches who had fought for the jug over the last 50 years. Photographs of Paul Giel, 1953 Minnesota captain, and Ed Rogers, 1903 captain, adorn the cover. (Ken Magee collection.)

Here is a 1953 season ticket and game program for the Little Brown Jug contest at Memorial Stadium. The Gophers shut out the Wolverines 22-0 to end a 10-year drought and win the Little Brown Jug. This game marked the 50th anniversary of the 1903 game, the birth year of the Little Brown Jug. (Both, Ken Magee collection.)

All-American tailback Paul Giel was a two-time All-American and the first two-time Big Ten Conference Most Valuable Player in 1952 and 1953. In the 1953 game, he single-handedly demolished the Wolverines with 112 rushing yards and 169 passing yards. He scored two of the three Gopher touchdowns while passing for another in the 22-0 shutout of the Wolverines. He later became athletic director of the University of Minnesota. He was inducted into the College Football Hall of Fame in 1975. His No. 10 was retired by the University of Minnesota in 1991. (UMA.)

Michigan tailback Ted Kress is shown running the ball against a formidable Minnesota defense in 1953. A year earlier, Kress set a new single-game Michigan rushing record of 218 yards, which broke the previous record of 216 yards set by Bill Daley in 1943. (*Michiganensian* yearbook.)

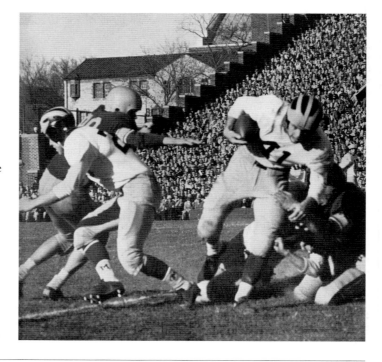

Head coach Murray Warmath arrived in Minnesota in 1954. Known for being a perfectionist and a firm believer in defense, he coached the Gophers until 1971. His crowning moment was the 1960 regular season, when his team was 8-1 and declared national champions despite subsequently losing in the Rose Bowl to Washington and ending the season with an 8-2 record. (UMA.)

Michigan quarterback Jim Maddock (left) and halfback Tony Branoff surround the Little Brown Jug with trainer Jim Hunt during the 1955 season. The Wolverines traveled to Minnesota that year and, in a thriller, came out on top 14-13. (BHL.)

Here is a 1956 ticket stub to the contest held in Michigan Stadium in front of a homecoming crowd. That season marked the first with Michigan's new press box, which towered over the 85,566 spectators in Michigan Stadium for the game. The Gophers upset the Wolverines 20-7 to earn the right to return to Minneapolis with the Little Brown Jug. (Ken Magee collection.)

Michigan Wolverine Mike Rotunno tackles Gopher star quarterback Bobby Cox. Cox scored two touchdowns in the 1956 matchup while running Minnesota's no-huddle offense. This strategy baffled Michigan, and Minnesota defeated the Wolverines soundly, 20-7. (*Michiganensian* yearbook.)

Future 1957 All-American halfback Jim Pace (left), teammate quarterback Jim Maddock, and trainer Jim Hunt of Michigan admire the Little Brown Jug, which was soon turned over to the Gophers after their 1956 victory. (*Michiganensian* yearbook.)

Coach Warmath celebrates with quarterback Bobby Cox and the Minnesota team after their 20-7 victory in 1956. (MVC.)

Coach Warmath (center) smiles at the jug with quarterbacks Dick Larson (left) and Bobby Cox. It was Coach Warmath's first victory against the Wolverines to win the Little Brown Jug. He went on to win it six more times. (UMA.)

LITTLE BROWN JUG DAY

MINNESOTA vs MICHIGAN

the Gopher Goalpost official program 25¢

JON JELACIC
Right End

memorial stadium
october 26, 1957

Shown is a 1957 game program for the matchup in Minnesota, which was proclaimed as "Little Brown Jug Day." The Wolverines scored 24 first-half points to ruin the homecoming celebration at Memorial Stadium. Michigan All-American halfback Jim Pace had a fantastic afternoon on the gridiron, scoring two touchdowns. (Ken Magee collection.)

Wolverine quarterback Jim Van Pelt runs with the football during the 1957 contest. Van Pelt outplayed highly touted Gopher quarterback Bobby Cox while tossing one touchdown pass and kicking three extra points and a field goal in front of 63,523 spectators. This led to a 24-7 Wolverine victory. (*Michiganensian* yearbook.)

Michigan quarterback Jim Van Pelt (left) and halfback Jim Pace (center) celebrate in the visitors' locker room at Memorial Stadium with legendary equipment manager Henry Hatch following the 1957 victory. (BHL.)

University of Michigan athletic director Fritz Crisler poses in front of the Little Brown Jug in 1957. (Ken Magee collection.)

1943–1968: THE BATTLE CONTINUES

Louis Elbel leads the Wolverines marching band in a rendition of Michigan's historic fight song "The Victors" during the 1958 homecoming game matchup against Minnesota at Michigan Stadium. Elbel wrote the fight song in 1898 while returning to Ann Arbor on a train after a Michigan upset victory over the University of Chicago Maroon. The 1958 homecoming game resulted in a thriller, with Michigan winning the Little Brown Jug 20-19. (*Michiganensian* yearbook.)

Michigan quarterback Bob Ptacek holds the Little Brown Jug after the 1958 game in Ann Arbor. The Wolverines did not disappoint the homecoming crowd of 72,591. The victory was coach Bennie Oosterbaan's final game against the Gophers. (BHL.)

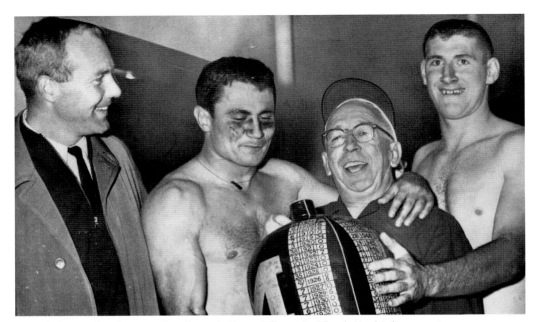

From left to right, first-year head coach Bump Elliott, halfback Fred Julian, equipment manager Henry Hatch, and halfback Darrell Harper celebrate Elliott's first victory over the Gophers by a score of 14-6 in 1959. Harper accounted for Michigan's first touchdown with an 83-yard punt return, and Julian also scored on a 42-yard rushing touchdown in front of a sold-out crowd in Memorial Stadium. (Ken Magee collection.)

This 1960s photograph shows a homecoming float on the Michigan campus. (BHL.)

Michigan's marching band forms the Little Brown Jug on the field at halftime of the 1960 game in Ann Arbor. The Gophers defeated the Wolverines 10-0 on their way to a national championship. (BHL.)

Members of the University of Michigan marching band proudly display the Little Brown Jug during the 1960 homecoming weekend in Ann Arbor before the Wolverines' loss to the Gophers. (Ken Magee collection.)

Minnesota guard Tom "Brownie" Brown was an All-American and Minnesota's first winner of the Outland Award. He took second place for the Heisman Trophy award and was an instrumental part of the 1960 University of Minnesota national champions. He was inducted into the College Football Hall of Fame in 2003. (UMA.)

Various Gophers celebrate with the Little Brown Jug as they return to Minnesota after the 1960 victory over the Wolverines. (UMA.)

Shown here is the 1960 national champion Minnesota team. The Gophers went 8-2 under Coach Warmath and 6-1 in the Big Ten Conference. They went on to lose the Rose Bowl to the Washington Huskies, 17-7. (UMA.)

This is one of the last photographs of Oscar Munson as he proudly holds the jug in 1960. Munson died later in 1960 at 81 years of age, just prior to the end of the 1960 football season. (MVC.)

This early-1960s float is seen on the campus of Minnesota for the homecoming parade. The float depicts a giant Gopher holding the Little Brown Jug. (UMA.)

Sandy Stephens was an All-American quarterback who played for the Gophers from 1959 to 1961. The 1961 matchup against the Wolverines was a thriller at Memorial Stadium. Stephens ran for a 63-yard touchdown and threw a 46-yard touchdown pass late in the fourth quarter that gave the Gophers the 23-20 victory and the Little Brown Jug. The Gophers went on to win the Rose Bowl, defeating UCLA 21-3. Stephens was inducted into the College Football Hall of Fame in 2011. His No. 15 was retired by the University of Minnesota in 2000. (UMA.)

This program is from the 1962 game, which saw Minnesota travel to Ann Arbor to defeat Michigan for the third consecutive year. Michigan gained only 50 yards on 66 plays. This resulted in a Minnesota 17-0 shutout and the Gophers taking the Little Brown Jug back to Minnesota. (Ken Magee collection.)

Bobby Lee Bell was a two-time All-American and winner of the 1962 Outland Award while playing tackle at the University of Minnesota. He was inducted into the College Football Hall of Fame in 1991. After his days on the Gopher campus, he went on to play professional football for the Kansas City Chiefs and won a Super Bowl ring by defeating the Minnesota Vikings. He was inducted into the Pro Football Hall of Fame in 1983. His No. 78 was retired by the University of Minnesota in 2010. (LJ.)

On the program cover, reading vertically: memorial stadium · · · october 26, 1963

HOMECOMING
WELCOME GRADS
**MINNESOTA
MICHIGAN**
GOPHER GOALPOST
OFFICIAL PROGRAM 35c

A 1963 game program depicts a large Gopher on a homecoming float hugging the Little Brown Jug, and rightfully so. Minnesota went on to win the Little Brown Jug for the fourth consecutive year by shutting out the Wolverines 6-0. This was the third shutout over the University of Michigan in four years. (Ken Magee collection.)

Carl Eller is pictured here leaping high in the air to block a pass in the 1963 game against Michigan. Eller, a defensive giant on the field, was an All-American in 1963 and went on to play many years for the Minnesota Vikings. He was inducted into the College Football Hall of Fame in 2006 and the Pro Football Hall of Fame in 2004. (LJ.)

This is a 1964 game-day program for the matchup in Ann Arbor. The late Henry Hatch, the legendary equipment manager for Michigan, is seen on the cover in a tribute to his years of service from 1921 to 1963 at Michigan. The Gophers made it close, but Michigan won 20-15. The Wolverines went on to win their first conference championship since 1950 and defeated Oregon State in the Rose Bowl 34-7. (Ken Magee collection.)

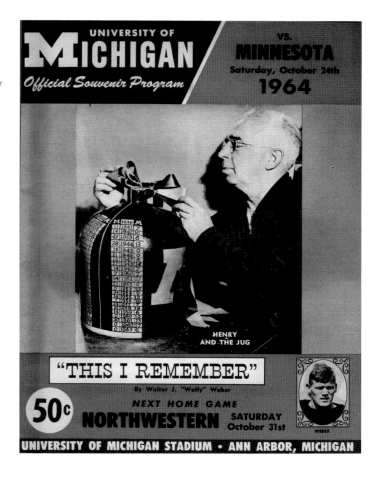

Coach Elliott, end Bill Laskey (No. 83), team captain and end Jim Conley (No. 82), All-American quarterback Bob Timberlake (second from right), and center Tom Cecchini (No. 53) celebrate the 1964 Michigan homecoming victory with the Little Brown Jug. The victory broke a four-game losing streak to the Gophers. (MVC.)

GOPHER GOALPOST   50¢

MINNESOTA

MICHIGAN

MEMORIAL STADIUM   OCT. 23, 1965

HOMECOMING

Shown here is the 1965 game program for the contest at Memorial Stadium in front of 55,519 spectators. The Gophers won in a wild one, 14-13. Michigan scored in the final minute and attempted a two-point conversion, which failed and secured the win for Minnesota. (Ken Magee collection.)

Triumphant Gophers carry the Little Brown Jug off the field in front of a hometown crowd after defeating Michigan in 1965. Minnesota had now won five of the last six games against the Wolverines. (CP.)

UNIVERSITY OF MICHIGAN

Official Souvenir Program

1966

MINNESOTA SATURDAY October 22nd

TOM HARMON

"THIS I REMEMBER"

By TOM HARMON

NEXT HOME GAME
ILLINOIS SATURDAY November 5th

50¢

HARMON

UNIVERSITY OF MICHIGAN STADIUM · ANN ARBOR, MICHIGAN

This 1966 game program depicts Michigan's legendary Tom Harmon. Harmon wrote the "This I Remember" section of the game program and reflected on his years at Michigan. Harmon wrote that he personally took responsibility for two of the three Michigan losses to Minnesota during his career. Harmon was proud of his alma mater this day, as the Wolverines unleashed an effective offense in front of 71,749 homecoming fans, winning 49-0. That weekend was the 70th-annual homecoming hosted by Michigan. (Ken Magee collection.)

Coach Elliott and All-American defensive back Rick Volk admire the Little Brown Jug in 1966. Volk was a great football athlete, playing various positions on both offense and defense. He was the nephew of Michigan All-American football legend Bob Chappuis, one of Michigan's "Mad Magicians" from 1947. Volk wore his uncle's uniform No. 49 during his entire 1964–1966 career at Michigan. He went on to play 12 seasons in the National Football League and won a Super Bowl ring with the Baltimore Colts in Super Bowl V. (BHL.)

Michigan All-American end and captain Jack Clancy, surrounded by teammates, holds the Little Brown Jug after Michigan's 1966 victory of 49-0. Clancy scored two touchdowns on passes from quarterback Dick Vidmer and overall had 10 receptions for 168 yards in one of his greatest games. (Ken Magee collection.)

In this c. 1965 photograph, Gopher student football manager Tim McGovern, nicknamed "the Governor," is standing with three Gopher rivalry trophies that the Gophers had won in the same year. The trophies are the Little Brown Jug, the Floyd of Rosedale Pig (in a rivalry with Iowa since 1935), and the Paul Bunyan Axe (in a rivalry with Wisconsin since 1948). The Gophers have only won all three trophies in the same year in 1960, 1965, and 1967. In 1993, Minnesota added the Governors Victory Bell trophy, going to the winner of the Penn State–Minnesota game. (LJ.)

Pictured is the 1968 game program for the homecoming game in Ann Arbor in front of a crowd of 69,384. The Wolverines won 33-20. Quarterback Dennis Brown threw two touchdowns, and All-American halfback Ron Johnson scored two more rushing touchdowns. This was the last time Coach Elliott would coach in the battle for the Little Brown Jug. (Ken Magee collection.)

Michigan quarterback Dennis Brown sets up to pass against the Gophers in the 33-20 victory for the Wolverines in front of a 1968 homecoming crowd. Michigan scored all 33 points in the first half, and Brown accounted for two touchdowns by passing to Paul Staroba and Billy Harris. (Ken Magee collection.)

Author Ken Magee, at age 10, shakes hands with Michigan All-American and captain Ron Johnson (in Crisler Arena) after Johnson received the *Chicago Tribune*'s Silver Football Trophy as the Big Ten Conference Player of the Year for the 1968 season. Ken's brother James, in the foreground (striped shirt), is waiting his turn to meet a Wolverine football legend. Johnson was a two-time team most valuable player, as well as a football legend who still holds Michigan's single game-rushing record of 347 yards against Wisconsin in 1968. (Ken Magee collection.)

6

1969 – PRESENT
MICHIGAN DOMINATES

With the arrival of new head coach Glenn Edward "Bo" Schembechler on the Ann Arbor campus in 1969, Michigan football started to take on a new but familiar look: winning championships. Schembechler led Michigan to 13 Big Ten Conference championships during his tenure and defeated the Gophers 19 times with only two losses. Schembechler and four subsequent head coaches have a combined record of 38-3 in the battle for the Little Brown Jug. Two of those losses to an inspired Gophers squad knocked Schembechler's heavily favored teams out of national championship contention. In the third loss, coach Glen Mason's Gophers upset future College Football Hall of Fame head coach Lloyd Carr's Wolverines in Ann Arbor on a last-second field goal. The Little Brown Jug can be an inspiration to either team as demonstrated by these upsets by the Gophers.

The Little Brown Jug can also motivate a team to accomplish something never done before, as seen in the 2003 Michigan historic come-from-behind victory against a Minnesota football program that had been demonstrating a resurgence. Michigan scored four touchdowns in the final quarter to erase a 21-point Minnesota lead, thus capping the greatest comeback in Michigan's 134 years of playing the sport. In his memoirs, Michigan football head coach Bo Schembechler wrote on the importance of the Little Brown Jug, "I never realized how much the jug meant until we lost it."

MINNESOTA MICHIGAN

"GOPHER GOALPOST"

EST. PRICE	.49¢
STATE TAX	.01¢
TOTAL	.50¢

50¢

UNIVERSITY OF MINNESOTA ■ MEMORIAL STADIUM ■ OCTOBER 25TH, 1969

LIL' BROWN JUG

ITS M DAY!

WELCOME TWIN CITY IRON RANGERS ASSOCIATION

This is a 1969 program for the Little Brown Jug game at Memorial Stadium. This contest introduced new Michigan head coach Bo Schembechler to the storied rivalry. Michigan trailed at halftime 9-7 after three Gopher field goals, but the Wolverines rebounded in the second half to win 35-9. Future 1971 All-American Billy Taylor was outstanding, having a breakout game by rushing for 151 yards and three touchdowns. It would be the first of Bo's 19 Little Brown Jug game victories. (Ken Magee collection.)

Coach Bo Schembechler crouches on the sideline at Michigan Stadium. This pose would become a familiar sight for 21 years to Michigan fans. Schembechler, a Michigan football legend, received numerous awards during his coaching career, beginning in 1969 with the NCAA Coach of the Year Award. Schembechler's overall record versus Minnesota in the battle for the Little Brown Jug was an outstanding 19-2. He was inducted into the College Football Hall of Fame in 1993. (RK-BHL.)

Michigan halfbacks Glenn Doughty (No. 22) and All-American Billy Taylor (No. 42) carry the Little Brown Jug in its trophy case after the 1971 game in Minneapolis. Taylor had another outstanding game against the Gophers, rushing for 166 yards and scoring two touchdowns in Michigan's 35-7 win. Also, this was the game where Taylor passed Ron Johnson as the all-time Michigan career leader in rushing yards. (BHL.)

This 1972 Michigan Stadium game program shows the Little Brown Jug on the cover. The Michigan homecoming crowd was treated well, as the Wolverines won 42-0. Michigan fullback Ed Shuttlesworth scored four touchdowns, which matched Fritz Seyferth's four touchdowns scored against Minnesota in 1970. Quarterback Dennis Franklin and All-American defensive back Dave Brown both added a touchdown in the 1972 game. (Ken Magee collection.)

Minnesota quarterback Tony Dungy was a talented player from 1973 through 1976. He was recruited out of the Wolverines backyard from Jackson, Michigan, near Ann Arbor. He was elected the team's most valuable player in 1975 and 1976 and was team captain in 1976. Dungy went on to have an outstanding career in professional football as a player and as head coach. As head coach for Indianapolis, he led the Colts to a Super Bowl victory in 2007. (UMA.)

Minnesota players in 1977 are joyfully hoisting the Little Brown Jug after their 16-0 upset of the no. 1 ranked Michigan Wolverines in Minneapolis. This was considered one of the biggest upsets in the storied history of the Little Brown Jug. The Gopher defense held Michigan to only 80 yards rushing. Minnesota place kicker Paul Rogind accounted for three field goals, and halfback Marion Barber ran for the only game touchdown for the Gophers. This was Coach Schembechler's first of two losses against the Gophers in his career. (UMAD.)

This 1978 Michigan homecoming game program features a photograph of a replica Little Brown Jug (note the jug's rounded handle) and the 1903 game football etched with the scores for both Minnesota and Michigan. It was the 75th anniversary of the historic 1903 tie game. Michigan won decisively, 42-10, as All-American Rick Leach accounted for all five Michigan touchdowns: two rushing and three passing. Freshman tailback and future 1981 All-American Butch Woolfolk ran 49 yards for the game's final touchdown. (Ken Magee collection.)

MICHIGAN

1903-1978

MINNESOTA

75 Years of Tradition

Homecoming 1978 ' Michigan Stadium ' Ann Arbor, Michigan ' Oct. 28, 1978 ' 1

Legendary Michigan end Ron Kramer (right) is seen at halftime of the 1978 homecoming game waving to Wolverine fans as he is presented his College Football Hall of Fame induction certificate alongside Michigan athletic director Don Canham. Kramer was a two-time All-American in 1955 and 1956. His No. 87 was retired by Michigan in 1956. He went on to have a memorable professional football career with the Green Bay Packers and Detroit Lions. (RK-BHL.)

THE LITTLE BROWN JUG: THE MICHIGAN-MINNESOTA FOOTBALL RIVALRY   119

Here is the 1982 Michigan homecoming game program; the Wolverines won 52-14. Michigan's attack featured quarterback Steve Smith and three-time All-American Anthony Carter. Smith passed for three touchdowns. Michigan proceeded to win its 10th Big Ten Conference championship in 14 years under Coach Schembechler. (Ken Magee collection.)

The 1987 game program cover depicts Minnesota field goal kicker Chip Lohmiller alongside coach John Gutekunst. The Little Brown Jug was in Minnesota's possession after the 1986 upset of the Wolverines. After that game, Coach Schembechler stated, "My hats off to Minnesota. They played a great game today. We made too many mistakes." Minnesota benefitted from five costly turnovers by heavily favored Michigan. Minnesota quarterback Rickey Foggie scampered to the Michigan 31-yard line late in the fourth quarter and set up Lohmiller's game-winning field goal as time expired, giving the Gophers a 20-17 victory. (Ken Magee collection.)

This is Minnesota running back Darrell Thompson, who played from 1986 to 1989, in a game-action photograph. He amassed 4,654 rushing yards to become the school's all-time leading rusher and also holds the team record of 40 career touchdowns. In the 1987 game, with the ball on their own two-yard line and holding a slim 10-7 lead over the Wolverines, sophomore Thompson took the handoff and raced 98 yards for the touchdown. This run would set the Big Ten Conference record for the longest run from scrimmage in a game. Michigan rebounded to win the game 30-20. (UMA.)

Michigan 1991 team captain, All-American, and Butkus Award–winning linebacker Erick Anderson raises the Little Brown Jug to celebrate visiting Michigan's win over Minnesota, 52-6. The Wolverines went on to win the Big Ten Conference under the leadership of head coach Gary Moeller. Michigan finished 10-2 but lost in the Rose Bowl to eventual national champion University of Washington. The team was led by Heisman trophy winner and All-American Desmond Howard and quarterback Elvis Grbac. (BHL.)

Michigan wide receiver and 1991 All-American Desmond Howard poses with head coach Gary Moeller. Howard's acrobatic catches made him one of the most electrifying players ever to play the college game. The All-American scored 23 touchdowns for Michigan in 1991. He also recorded 19 consecutive career games with a scoring catch. Desmond Howard won the Heisman Trophy in 1991 by a large margin of victory. Moeller coached at Michigan from 1990 to 1994 and was 5-0 against the Gophers. (Ken Magee collection.)

Legendary equipment manager Jon Falk is seen here with the Little Brown Jug in 1997. In 2014, he retired after completing 40 years of service to the Michigan football program. Hired by Bo Schembechler in 1974, Falk embraced the tradition and history of Michigan football so much that he became part of it himself. Quotes Falk, "I remember the day that Bo interviewed me and said that working at the University of Michigan would present great opportunities for my career." Schembechler was correct, as Falk participated in Michigan's 1997 undefeated national championship season. (BHL.)

Michigan defensive backs Marcus Ray (No. 29) and Charles Woodson (No. 2) celebrate with the Little Brown Jug after a 24-3 victory. The 1997 homecoming game saw the no. 1–ranked defense in the country allow only an early field goal. All-American and 1997 Heisman Trophy winner Charles Woodson, playing on offense, provided a spark, scoring on a reverse in the second quarter. Michigan, behind the strength of its defense and quarterback Brian Griese's passing, went on to win the national championship under the leadership of head coach Lloyd Carr by defeating Washington State in the Rose Bowl 21-16. (CP.)

Michigan end Andy Mignery lifts the Little Brown Jug in 2003. The Gophers had built a 28-7 lead by the end of the third quarter. Michigan quarterback John Navarre, All-American running back Chris Perry, and All-American wide receiver Braylon Edwards responded with four touchdowns in the fourth quarter, capped by place kicker Garrett Rivas's 33-yard field goal with 47 seconds left to win 38-35. The game was dubbed the "Miracle in the Metrodome" and was Michigan's greatest comeback victory of all time, accomplished on the 100-year anniversary of the 1903 game. (Photograph by Eric Bronson, courtesy of wolverinephoto.com.)

Minnesota players celebrate their 23-20 victory in Ann Arbor in 2005. Coach Glen Mason's Minnesota Gophers were led by captain, All-American, and 2005 Outland Award–winner center Greg Eslinger, quarterback Bryan Cupito, and running backs Laurence Maroney and Gary Russell. In a close game that was tied late in the fourth quarter, Russell ran 61 yards to set up a field goal situation. Jason Giannini kicked a 30-yard, game-winning field goal with one second remaining. For the jubilant Gophers, the 2005 Little Brown Jug victory was their first win in the series dating back to 1986. (JA-BHL.)

First-year Michigan head coach Brady Hoke and defensive end Ryan Van Bergen raise the Little Brown Jug in celebration of a 58-0 whitewashing of Minnesota in the 2011 game. This resulted in Michigan's largest margin of victory in the series to date. Also, this game marked the first Big Ten Conference game for Coach Hoke and spring-boarded Michigan to an 11-2 overall record and a BCS Sugar Bowl overtime victory over Virginia Tech, 23-20. (MVC.)

Michigan defensive end Ryan Van Bergen parades the Little Brown Jug around Michigan Stadium, much to the delight of the frenzied Wolverine faithful after Michigan's 2011 victory over the Gophers. (JK.)

Jil Gordon paints the final score on the Little Brown Jug in 2013. This event took place after the Wolverines 42-13 victory in Michigan Stadium, marking the 100th game between the two schools. Jil painted the game scores on the Little Brown Jug several times in the early 1980s for her dear friend and legendary Michigan equipment manager Jon Falk. Upon returning to Ann Arbor in 2002, she resumed this "sacred privilege." Jil stated, "I feel so privileged to do something so simple, but yet so significant. It is continuing Michigan history, and not many are given a special task like this. Painting the score on the oldest collegiate rivalry trophy—but for Michigan." (MVC.)

SERIES RECORD

DATE	WINNER	SCORE	SITE	ATTENDANCE
Oct. 17, 1892	Minnesota	14-6	Minneapolis	-
Oct. 28, 1893	Minnesota	34-20	Ann Arbor	
Nov. 23, 1895	Michigan	20-0	Detroit	3,500
Nov. 07, 1896	Michigan	6-4	Minneapolis	-
Nov. 13, 1897	Michigan	14-0	Detroit	-
Nov. 27, 1902	Michigan	23-6	Ann Arbor	9,000
*Oct. 31, 1903	Tie	6-6	Minneapolis	20,000
Nov. 20, 1909	Michigan	15-6	Minneapolis	22,000
Nov. 19, 1910	Michigan	6-0	Ann Arbor	18,000
Nov. 22, 1919	Minnesota	34-7	Ann Arbor	30,000
Nov. 20, 1920	Michigan	3-0	Minneapolis	22,000
Nov. 19, 1921	Michigan	38-0	Ann Arbor	30,000
Nov. 25, 1922	Michigan	16-7	Minneapolis	20,000
Nov. 24, 1923	Michigan	10-0	Ann Arbor	42,000
Nov. 01, 1924	Michigan	13-0	Minneapolis	50,000
Nov. 21, 1925	Michigan	35-0	Ann Arbor	47,000
Oct. 16, 1926	Michigan	20-0	Ann Arbor	48,000
Nov. 20, 1926	Michigan	7-6	Minneapolis	55,000
Nov. 19, 1927	Minnesota	13-7	Ann Arbor	84,423
Nov. 16, 1929	Michigan	7-6	Minneapolis	58,160
Nov. 15, 1930	Michigan	7-0	Ann Arbor	54,944
Nov. 21, 1931	Michigan	6-0	Ann Arbor	37,251
Nov. 19, 1932	Michigan	3-0	Minneapolis	24,766
Nov. 18, 1933	Tie	0-0	Ann Arbor	51,137
Nov. 03, 1934	Minnesota	34-0	Minneapolis	59,362
Nov. 16, 1935	Minnesota	40-0	Ann Arbor	32,029
Oct. 17, 1936	Minnesota	26-0	Minneapolis	41,209
Oct. 16, 1937	Minnesota	39-6	Ann Arbor	53,266
Oct. 15, 1938	Minnesota	7-6	Minneapolis	54,212
Nov. 11, 1939	Minnesota	20-7	Ann Arbor	66,572
Nov. 09, 1940	Minnesota	7-6	Minneapolis	60,481
Oct. 25, 1941	Minnesota	7-0	Ann Arbor	84,658
Oct. 24, 1942	Minnesota	16-14	Minneapolis	49,181
Oct. 23, 1943	Michigan	49-6	Ann Arbor	42,966
Oct. 07, 1944	Michigan	28-13	Minneapolis	37,256
Nov. 03, 1945	Michigan	26-0	Ann Arbor	84,472
Nov. 02, 1946	Michigan	21-0	Minneapolis	58,476
Oct. 25, 1947	Michigan	13-6	Ann Arbor	85,938
Oct. 23, 1948	Michigan	27-14	Minneapolis	64,076
Oct. 22, 1949	Michigan	14-7	Ann Arbor	97,239
Oct. 28, 1950	Tie	7-7	Minneapolis	59,412
Oct. 27, 1951	Michigan	54-27	Ann Arbor	83,060
Oct. 25, 1952	Michigan	21-0	Ann Arbor	72,404
Oct. 24, 1953	Minnesota	22-0	Minneapolis	62,795
Oct. 23, 1954	Michigan	34-0	Ann Arbor	70,740
Oct. 22, 1955	Michigan	14-13	Minneapolis	63,530
Oct. 27, 1956	Minnesota	20-7	Ann Arbor	85,566
Oct. 26, 1957	Michigan	24-7	Minneapolis	63,523
Oct. 25, 1958	Michigan	20-19	Ann Arbor	72,591
Oct. 24, 1959	Michigan	14-6	Minneapolis	56,082

Date	Winner	Score	Location	Attendance
Oct. 22, 1960	Minnesota	10-0	Ann Arbor	71,752
Oct. 28, 1961	Minnesota	23-20	Minneapolis	63,898
Oct. 27, 1962	Minnesota	17-0	Ann Arbor	65,484
Oct. 26, 1963	Minnesota	6-0	Minneapolis	51,088
Oct. 24, 1964	Michigan	19-12	Ann Arbor	61,859
Oct. 23, 1965	Minnesota	14-13	Minneapolis	55,519
Oct. 22, 1966	Michigan	49-0	Ann Arbor	71,749
Oct. 28, 1967	Minnesota	20-15	Minneapolis	50,006
Oct. 26, 1968	Michigan	33-20	Ann Arbor	69,384
Oct. 25, 1969	Michigan	35-9	Minneapolis	44,028
Oct. 24, 1970	Michigan	39-13	Ann Arbor	83,496
Oct. 23, 1971	Michigan	35-7	Minneapolis	44,176
Oct. 28, 1972	Michigan	42-0	Ann Arbor	84,190
Oct. 27, 1973	Michigan	34-7	Minneapolis	44,435
Oct. 26, 1974	Michigan	49-0	Ann Arbor	96,284
Nov. 01, 1975	Michigan	28-21	Minneapolis	33,191
Oct. 30, 1976	Michigan	45-0	Ann Arbor	104,426
Oct. 22, 1977	Minnesota	16-0	Minneapolis	44,165
Oct. 28, 1978	Michigan	42-10	Ann Arbor	105,308
Oct. 13, 1979	Michigan	31-21	Ann Arbor	104,677
Oct. 18, 1980	Michigan	37-14	Minneapolis	56,297
Oct. 31, 1981	Michigan	34-13	Minneapolis	52,875
Oct. 30, 1982	Michigan	52-14	Ann Arbor	105,619
Nov. 12, 1983	Michigan	58-10	Minneapolis	40,945
Nov. 10, 1984	Michigan	31-7	Ann Arbor	101,247
Nov. 16, 1985	Michigan	48-7	Minneapolis	64,129
Nov. 15, 1986	Minnesota	20-17	Ann Arbor	104,864
Nov. 07, 1987	Michigan	30-20	Minneapolis	55,481
Nov. 05, 1988	Michigan	22-7	Ann Arbor	102,171
Nov. 18, 1989	Michigan	49-15	Minneapolis	35,103
Nov. 17, 1990	Michigan	35-18	Ann Arbor	102,112
Oct. 25, 1991	Michigan	52-6	Minneapolis	32,577
Oct. 24, 1992	Michigan	63-13	Ann Arbor	106,579
Nov. 13, 1993	Michigan	58-7	Minneapolis	44,603
Nov. 12, 1994	Michigan	38-22	Ann Arbor	105,624
Oct. 28, 1995	Michigan	52-17	Ann Arbor	104,929
Oct. 26, 1996	Michigan	44-10	Minneapolis	41,246
Nov. 01, 1997	Michigan	24-3	Ann Arbor	106,577
Oct. 31, 1998	Michigan	15-10	Minneapolis	41,310
Nov. 10, 2001	Michigan	31-10	Ann Arbor	110,828
Nov. 09, 2002	Michigan	41-24	Minneapolis	53,773
Oct. 10, 2003	Michigan	38-35	Minneapolis	62,374
Oct. 09, 2004	Michigan	27-24	Ann Arbor	111,518
Oct. 08, 2005	Minnesota	23-20	Ann Arbor	111,117
Sept. 30, 2006	Michigan	28-14	Minneapolis	50,805
Oct. 27, 2007	Michigan	34-10	Ann Arbor,	109,432
Nov. 08, 2008	Michigan	29-6	Minneapolis	55,040
Oct. 01, 2011	Michigan	58-0	Ann Arbor	111,106
Nov. 03, 2012	Michigan	35-13	Minneapolis	48,801
Oct. 05, 2013	Michigan	42-13	Ann Arbor	111,079

*The Wolverines left the Little Brown Jug behind after this game

Current 100-game series: Michigan, 73 wins; Minnesota, 24 wins; 3 ties

DISCOVER THOUSANDS OF LOCAL HISTORY BOOKS FEATURING MILLIONS OF VINTAGE IMAGES

Arcadia Publishing, the leading local history publisher in the United States, is committed to making history accessible and meaningful through publishing books that celebrate and preserve the heritage of America's people and places.

Find more books like this at
www.arcadiapublishing.com

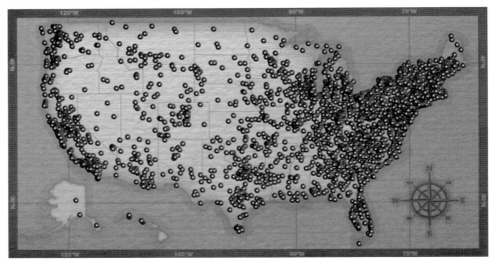

Search for your hometown history, your old stomping grounds, and even your favorite sports team.